NILES PUBLIC LIBRARY

Niles, Illinois

FINE SCHEDULE

Adult Materials . . . . 10 per day
Juvenile Materials . . . . . . 04 per day
Video Tapes . . . . . . $1.50 per day

A
PERSONAL
WAR
IN VIETNAM

TEXAS A&M UNIVERSITY
☆ 13 ☆
MILITARY HISTORY SERIES

A PERSONAL WAR IN VIETNAM

BY ROBERT FLYNN

TEXAS A&M UNIVERSITY PRESS
College Station

The paper used in this book meets the minimum
requirements of the American National Standard
for Permanence of Paper for Printed Library Materials, Z39.48-1984. Binding materials have been
chosen for durability.

Library of Congress Cataloging-in-Publication Data

Flynn, Robert, 1932–
    A personal war in Vietnam / by Robert
Flynn. — 1st ed.
        p.   cm. — (Texas A&M University
military history series ; no. 13)
        ISBN 0-89096-407-6 (alk. paper). —
ISBN 0-89096-418-1 (pbk. : alk. paper)
        1. Vietnamese Conflict, 1961–1975 —
Personal narratives, American.   2. Flynn,
Robert, 1932–   . I. Title. II. Series: Texas
A&M University military history series ; 13.
DS559.5.F59   1989
959.704'38 — dc19   89-4630
                                               CIP

To the men of Golf CUPP, the Fifth Marines,
and all those who served

Contents

Introduction

I had many reasons for going to Vietnam, none of them entirely satisfactory. I was almost thirty-eight years old, a husband and a father, a novelist and a professor, and a former Marine.

Many of my fellow citizens were engaged in an intense and arduous struggle. Many others were engaged in an intense and arduous opposition to that struggle. It was a momentous, soul-splitting, nation-tearing experience, almost certainly the most momentous experience of my lifetime. I did not intend to be on the sidelines, immune to the moral and physical difficulties, exempt from the moral and physical pain, of those who were engaged.

Like others, I was trying to understand Vietnam, and I found the government's reasons for being there and the war protestors' reasons for leaving more confusing than convincing. Equally confusing were the reports of what was happening—a firefight here, a bombing there, a shelling in some other town or village or province. The news—indeed the war—seemed without coherence, cohesion, focus, or, as far as I could tell, strategy. I wanted to know.

There was also a shadowy reason not clearly understood even today. I had been a Marine. I had dropped out of college to enlist during the Korean peace action. I expected and intended to go to Korea, to fight for my country or whatever the rationale was, and I expected to be confirmed and transformed by the experience, the way some women expect to be confirmed and transformed by childbirth. I would be a man, but a man who understood what manhood meant, who knew the limits of his courage and endurance, who had looked life and death in the eye and would never again be afraid of anything—the flinty-eyed hero I had seen in war and western movies.

I never got to Korea. I got to a replacement draft, went through infantry training, and then, when the others got shipping orders to Korea, I got orders to a range company at Camp Pendleton. I was a Marine, even a wartime Marine, who had served during but not in Korea, and I had boot-camp stories to tell, but I had not been confirmed, and I had not been transformed. And I was not flinty eyed.

In addition, I had an idea for a novel about the sole survivor of a military disaster, and it seemed necessary to go to Vietnam in order to research the book. Anyone could go to South Vietnam; all you needed was a visa and an airline ticket to Saigon. The problem wasn't getting there; the problem was getting around the country. There was a mother who visited her son in the field, and a man who went into the countryside looking for his brother who was missing in action, but as a general rule it was best to travel around the country in military vehicles and in the company of armed troops. That required press credentials.

My next step was to ask my agent to get me an assignment to Vietnam. With a monumental show of lethargy he asked a couple of magazines, I think *Esquire* and *New Yorker*, if they would like to send me to Vietnam to write some stories. They responded with a monumental show of disinterest. They already had reporters in Vietnam, thank you, who were serving them faithfully and well.

I don't know how far I would have carried it, but I did go to the Marine recruiting office in San Antonio to inquire about my country's need for me. The recruiting officer took one look at my Military Occupation Specialty—basic rifleman—and said my country could do very well without me, but thanks for dropping by and bringing a few laughs on a slow afternoon.

I decided to try something on my own. I remembered that a couple of years earlier *True* magazine had cited my novel *North to Yesterday* as one of the year's best. I sent them a copy of their review with a letter explaining my interest in going to Vietnam and writing stories about the men who were serving there. To my surprise, an assistant editor from *True* called to say they were interested and to come to New York and talk to them. About three weeks later, so quickly that my immunizations were overlapping, I was on my way to Vietnam.

My time in Vietnam was spent almost entirely in I (Eye) Corps.

I spent time with both the Army and the Marines but admit a bias toward the Marines. To the Army I was always a reporter, the subject of carefully disguised fear and contempt. I was treated with deference and suspicion, but always treated very well, even the grunts giving me the best they had. Once the Marines learned I had been a Marine, they considered me one of them, and the first question after blood type and zap number was what weapon did I want to carry?

After about two months in Vietnam I returned home. I was not greeted with open hostility the way many of the veterans were. I was greeted with denial. I met a concerted effort to deny that a place like Vietnam ever existed, that an experience like Vietnam ever happened, and an even more vehement denial that I knew anything about it. Both those who supported and those who opposed the war wanted to hear nothing about the war, whether it confirmed or contradicted their opinions. Their minds had not only been made up, they had been sealed. No one wanted reality intruding into their lives of self-interest and entertainment.

When I returned to my classes at the college, neither professors nor students wanted to hear about Vietnam. When, in an incautious moment, I did speak of Vietnam, they refused to believe that I, or veterans who served in Vietnam, knew anything about it. The only experts were those who had never been there. Only once was I invited to speak about Vietnam and that was to a church group. The members of the group were courteous but could hardly endure my words and fled at the first opportunity.

More important, no one wanted to read about Vietnam. *True* magazine did not use any of the stories I wrote. The longest of the stories, "Golf CUPP," was book-length, so I sent it to my publisher. The editor of my novels was complimentary but begged me not to publish the manuscript because no one wanted to read about Vietnam; the book would not sell and would damage my reputation with booksellers.

I put "Golf CUPP" on the shelf, where it remained for fifteen years. In 1987, I was working on a novel set in Vietnam and decided to read "Golf CUPP" to see if there was any information I could use for the novel. In reading the book, I saw that my judgment was fallible, my insight limited, my eyesight dull, and my interest and emphasis were sometimes in the wrong place. I also thought the book deserved to be published. As I knew of the excellent reputation of Texas A&M University Press's Military History Series, I sent the book to the director, Lloyd Lyman.

It was important to me that the book not be rewritten with the advantage of hindsight. I had recorded the conversations as they were spoken, I had described the actions shortly after they took place, and I had written the book directly after my return home from the notes and observations I had made in the field. These are the judgments I made at the time and on the scene with incomplete and sometimes misleading information. But the men I was writing about were also acting with incomplete and sometimes misleading information, and as I judged them for their on-the-spot decisions, I think I must allow others to judge me the same way. Lloyd Lyman and Texas A&M University Press agreed, and the only changes in the text, except for adding this Introduction, are due to copyediting.

I believe I was confirmed by my experience in Vietnam, although two decades later it is still not clear what was confirmed, and I was transformed, but in a way I had never imagined. I spent more time in the field with small combat units than some who did two or more tours in Saigon or Da Nang. Even so, I suffered an infinitesimal share of the fear, danger, and suffering of the men in those small combat units. In addition, I had the comfort of knowing that if I got myself into a dangerous situation, the military would do everything they could to get me out, and there would be no stigma of cowardice or desertion attached. And no matter what went wrong, I would be blamed for nothing.

Nevertheless, and despite my limited experience, I am still affected by a wariness, a fear of being caught off-guard. I still have nightmares, and incredibly, I have had a few flashbacks.

I returned home, after two months instead of the usual twelve, and everything had changed. I knew that even in America things didn't happen that quickly and that what had changed was my perception. Even so, it took me a few years to realize that I was filled with rage. A rage at the self-satisfaction of those who thought they knew and refused to hear. A rage at those who profited from the war, one that went far beyond politicians and defense contractors. To those coming home from the war, almost everyone who didn't go to Vietnam seemed to have profited from it. They had cars, girlfriends, clothes, jobs, health, happiness; they were surrounded by friends and memories of good times.

I had a special rage for those who profited by prolonging and expanding the myths of drug-crazed soldiers killing and raping, and war-crazed veterans becoming criminals. There were drugs in Vietnam, but there were drugs in America too. The only drugs I saw were in rear areas, and I saw more drugs on the college campus than I did in Vietnam.

Vietnam was a source of stress to soldiers whether they were there, preparing to go there, or had returned after serving there. No doubt some were crazed by it. I knew a couple of teenagers who had personality problems when they were in high school, and I wasn't surprised that service in Vietnam didn't cure those problems. I knew a few men who were in Vietnam because they had been given a choice between the Army and jail. I wasn't surprised that they were disciplinary problems in Vietnam and that after their return they made headlines such as "Vietnam vet robs liquor store." Vietnam destroyed many lives, both of those who went and of those who stayed behind. Dare we hope that a few have become better human beings because of their service?

The combat veterans must have felt a far greater rage than I. Rage at what they had done. Rage at what they had been asked to do. Rage at the ideals, the dreams, the hopes that had been blown away. Rage against the elements, the squalor of their living, the sordidness of their dying. Rage at the time they had lost from their youth, from their families, from the pursuit of their careers. Rage at their lost innocence, that their eyes had been opened to things they would see forever in their minds, that their ears had heard sounds human ears had hoped never to hear again. Rage that no tongue can ever tell, or should ever tell; rage at all they thought, felt, knew, became, and refused to be.

I suspect most veterans of most wars experience rage, but how angry can you be when citizens throw flowers when you pass by, call you noble and heroic for the horrors you have done, and thank you for serving them? But when your fellow citizens ask you to do something and, after you have done it, call you "baby killer" and worse, what antidote is there to rage? When citizens howl of the suffering you have cost them, of the dishonor you have brought upon them, what vessel is there to contain your rage?

No doubt some of it was the "movie mentality" that says all our causes are just and all our soldiers are heroes and that those who don't have to kill or be killed and don't have to endure fear, pain, and guilt will be eternally grateful to those who do.

But that doesn't explain my rage. My country didn't ask me to go; my country asked only that I, and my fellow citizens, assume responsibility for the lives and actions of those who did go. I wasn't one of them, and I shared only the least of their danger and discomfort. Maybe that's why it took me so long to recognize my rage, even longer to admit it. I didn't become an alcoholic, take drugs, commit crimes, or hit anybody. I buried the rage inside.

Having seen what was expected, even required, of eighteen- and twenty-year-olds in Vietnam, I was annoyed at how little colleges demanded of students and how little students expected of themselves. I had little patience for news reports of dead and wounded, and little tolerance for those who publicly wept on cue. I had a distinct distaste for bureaucratic featherbedding and looking out for number one. I had a revulsion for those who claimed the war righteous, and for those who claimed this war was bad but other wars had been good wars in which only bad people had been killed. I had contempt for those who said stop the killing when they meant stop the cameras so we can forget the killing and dying. I was repulsed by violence and destruction, particularly voyeuristic violence and destruction for the entertainment of the masses and the profit of the few.

The biggest change was my loss of certitude both as a writer and as a professor. Things have never seemed as simple as before I went to Vietnam. Regrettably, my country has never seemed as righteous, its causes as just.

I suppose it is inevitable that I draw some conclusions, although I am not a historian and know nothing of global strategy or politics. Neither the politicians nor the generals ever defined victory in the context of Vietnam. I think the war was winnable if victory was defined as a divided country as in Germany or Korea. I believe it would be hard to convince anyone who was in Vietnam in 1970 or 1971 that that war had not been won and that nothing short of the direct intervention of the Army of North Vietnam could prevent the defeat of the Viet Cong by the ARVN and the Regional and Popular Forces.

The killing would have gone on as NVA troops infiltrated from Laos and Cambodia. There would have been grenades in crowded theaters, mines under busloads of peasants. Burned and mutilated bodies would have remained the staple of television news, but Saigon, Hue, and Da Nang would have been safer than New York, Los Angeles, and Houston.

The eventual collapse of the ARVN will have to be explained by those familiar with the military and political history of Vietnam. But faced with the boat people, few can say that the South Vietnamese didn't care about freedom, that they preferred Communism, or that they trusted the minions of Ho Chi Minh. Some Americans secretly applauded when the Army of North Vietnam overran South Vietnam. Many were relieved. The bamboo curtain came down, and no longer did the flaming villages appear on television to inflict us with guilt and pain, to disrupt our pursuit of comfort and entertainment. It was a relief not to know.

I don't think America became involved in Vietnam for evil or dishonorable reasons. I believe our involvement in Vietnam was the result of political decisions, based in part on bad information, and that the domino theory is most clearly seen in the line of presidents. Truman leaned, Eisenhower wobbled, Kennedy fell.

I think the outcome would have been no different if John F. Kennedy had lived. I think if Robert Kennedy had been elected president, or Eugene McCarthy, he would have done almost precisely the same as Richard Nixon did. It is not easy for any man, even a president, to resist momentum once the dominoes start to fall.

Nor do I think all the dominoes have fallen or that we have learned any lessons. I believe President Ronald Reagan tipped, and that President Bush will be hard put not to topple. Americans persist in seeing themselves as the Lone Ranger who rides into town, chases out the bad men, and rides away while men cheer and virgins swoon. However, it becomes increasingly difficult to find Tonto.

The flinty-eyed hero who knows no fear is a sham, a threadbare actor facing down convenient and politically constructed enemies.

The men in Golf CUPP were scared. They faced their fear

every day and every night. They did what their country asked them to do, and they could teach all of us a lesson in facing patiently and heroically disasters of the daily variety. I hope this book will be another piece of the puzzle that was Vietnam and that in a small way it will be a vindication of all those who served.

Abbreviations

AO	Aerial observer
AOP	Area of Operation
ARVN	Army of the Republic of Vietnam
B.A.R.	Browning Automatic Rifle
BDA	Bomb Damage Assessment
C.O.	Commanding Officer; Conscientious Objector
C.P.	Command Post
C4	Composition Four (plastic explosive)
CUPP	Combined Unit Pacification Program
DMZ	Demilitarized Zone
EOD	Explosive Ordnance Demolition
FAC	Forward Air Control
JUSPAO	Joint U.S. Public Affairs Office
KT	Killer Team
LAW	Light Artillery Weapon (one-shot bazooka)
LZ	Landing Zone
MAC-V	Military Assistance Command, Vietnam
NCO	Noncommissioned Officer
NVA	North Vietnamese Army
PAO	Public Affairs Office
PF	Popular Forces (South Vietnam)
PFC	Private First Class
PSDF	Popular Self-Defense Forces
PX	Post Exchange
QL 1	National Highway One
R and R	Rest and Recreation
RF	Regional Forces (South Vietnam)
ROK	Republic of Korea
RPG	Rocket-Propelled Grenade

STOL	Short Takeoff and Landing
VC	Viet Cong
VMO	Marine Observation Squadron
WA	Wounded in Action

Glossary

Alley Cat	ambush
boo coo	best or most (corruption of French *beaucoup*)
cacadow	die
Chicom	Chinese Communist grenade
chieu hoi	open arms (i.e., return to the Saigon government)
day pos	day position
di-di	go
di-di mou	get out
dien cai dau	crazy
frag	fragmentation grenade
grunt	infantryman
gungy	corruption of *gung ho*
hoi chanh	defector
hootch	house, usually constructed of straw and bamboo
illum	illumination (i.e., flares)
joss sticks	incense
lau dai	come here
medevac	medical evacuation
mustang	officer from the ranks rather than from a military academy or college ROTC program
no bit	I don't understand
nook	rain
nuoc mam	fermented fish sauce

one-digit midget	someone due to leave Vietnam in less than ten days
Oscar Mike	on the move
papasan, mamasan, babysan	man, woman, child (form of address borrowed from Japanese)
song	river
TT	short, small
ville	hamlets that are numbered and together form a political unit—the village
willie peter	white phosphorus
zap number	military identification number, used for identification when a soldier is hit, or "zapped"

A PERSONAL WAR IN VIETNAM

Third Platoon

The jeep trip from Da Nang to Combat Base Baldy, headquarters of the Second Battalion, Fifth Marines, was supposed to have started early in the day but was delayed in Da Nang by the Bob Hope show. It was Christmas Eve, and the normally heavy Da Nang traffic had come to a standstill because of the heavy influx of military trucks carrying enlisted men to the Hope show and because of the added security measures that were being taken.

The trip was further delayed by a dead girl who lay in a pool of blood in the middle of a dirt road southwest of Hoi An. The jeep driver, S. Sgt. "Stony" Merriman, placed his M-16 across his knees and kept going. "This is Indian country," he said.

For the next few miles an occasional single Marine could be seen standing beside the road in his helmet and flak jacket, his rifle in his hand, waiting for the platoon jeep to bring food, ammunition, mail. "Those are CUPP Marines," Merriman said. The Marines were what I had come to see.

"It's a personal war to the CUPP teams," Lt. Frank Waldrop had told me. CUPP was the acronym for Combined Unit Pacification Program and referred to mixed teams of Marines and Vietnamese Popular Forces. Lieutenant Waldrop was the Public Affairs officer of the First Marine Division with an office in Da Nang, a relatively safe and comfortable city in a country where safety and comfort were always relative. In Da Nang the war was fought from charts and graphs and maps. In the way that MAC-V in Saigon was Pentagon East, Da Nang was MAC-V North.

Modern war has become increasingly a war of charts and graphs, telephones and buttons. The war in Vietnam more so than most. Men fought an unseen enemy for an abstract cause at nameless LZs, temporary base camps, fire bases, mountains, and jungles for goals which had not been precisely defined. Men at fire-support bases and men in airplanes supported men on the ground. Sometimes they accidentally killed those men on the ground, sometimes they saved them, more often they simply aided them in response to signals and sounds that crackled over radios and radiotelephones. For those few minutes or hours they were intensely united with men whom they had never and would never see; communicating with frightened, even dying, men who were strangers, even foreigners, bound for a moment by the thread of life that existed only in the earphones.

Modern war has become increasingly like that, where killers and saviors do their job without ever asking who or what, perhaps without wanting to know who or what. Nevertheless, the foot soldier has traditionally shared a bond of common danger and terror in a unit. Although individuals died, the unit remained, and the survivors identified with the unit. Even the dead and wounded were identified with the unit. In Vietnam even the smallest units were impersonal, the men known to each other not by their names but by nicknames. The unit stayed in Vietnam, the men rotated in and out of it like replaceable parts, so that at any given time there was likely to be a new man in the unit. The security of the unit often depended at least in part on the faithfulness, courage, reliability, and skill of a stranger. In Vietnam it wasn't the regiment one believed in, or the battalion, or even the platoon. It was the buddy. Most grunts were tight with a handful of buddies, some no more than one.

I was a thirty-eight-year-old writer and college professor in Vietnam as a correspondent for *True* magazine, looking for stories about men doing their jobs under arduous, even dangerous circumstances. There was another reason that I hadn't explained to anyone, or thought out very carefully to myself. War had been the dominant experience of my lifetime. All I remembered of the news of Pearl Harbor was the reaction of the adults; I was too young to have any reaction of my own. I saw Guadalcanal, Iwo Jima, and Omaha Beach; Spitfires, Corsairs, and B-17s in newsreels and movies. I saw trains carrying waving, smiling troops across the land. And I saw medaled heroes and Gold Star Mothers.

I was of age when North Korea invaded South Korea, and I

enlisted in the Marines and saw the war from Camp Pendleton while others were assigned to replacement drafts for training and transportation to front-line units. I had volunteered for combat, had been assigned to a replacement draft, and had been left behind at Camp Pendleton.

Now again, American troops were on foreign shores, and I was watching the news, reading the papers, and wondering what it was all about. This time I was determined to be a part of it, or at least to understand, and the only way I had found to be there was to write stories about men doing their job.

I had been at a remote firebase on the DMZ where men fired eight-inch shells at North Vietnam by some design unknown to the gunners, who went about their work with the precision and disinterest of ticket punchers. I had ridden in a guntruck that escorted truck convoys over the Hai Van Pass and up QL 1 to Phu Bai with a crew that was fiercely defensive of the truck drivers and totally indifferent to the other travelers on the highway, the villagers in the hamlets, and the peasants in the fields. Anyone who was not an enemy or a member of their unit was outside their interest.

I had seen men doing their jobs with skill and courage, but I had not seen involvement or commitment to anything beyond the immediate unit.

"The CUPP teams live with the Vietnamese people," Waldrop had said. "They play with the kids. A lot of them are on their second or third tour because they feel they have an investment in the ville." He told of one enlisted Marine who was getting out of the Corps so that he could stay in Vietnam. The Marines had refused him another tour. "He feels he has too much at stake here to leave," Waldrop explained.

Lieutenant Waldrop was handsome, big jawed, and intelligent. A former enlisted man, he had become an officer by attending Officers Candidate School through the Meritorious NCO program. He had spent some time as a reporter for *Stars and Stripes*, served as a line officer in Vietnam, learned the Thai language, and returned to Vietnam for a second tour as an Intelligence and Interrogation officer before being sent to the Public Affairs Office on the hill. "I won't give you a lot of bullshit," he said. "Go see for yourself."

I was intrigued by the small and personal war the Marines

were waging, and I was going to see for myself. Along the road we were traveling I could see an occasional Marine, but I could not see the villes in which they lived. Even after Sergeant Merriman pointed them out to me, I could hardly find the tiny hamlets, not far from the road, that were almost completely hidden in the trees or tucked into the folds of the land. That was the first correction I had to make in the mental image of Vietnam I had formed.

Combat Base Baldy I could spot from some distance by the wire, radio antenna, and the bare red earth. Baldy was a collection of barren hilltops, sandbagged hootches, and a metal-strip runway surrounded by barbed wire and bunkers. Atop one of the small hills was the Combat Operations Center of Golf CUPP, and inside the sandbagged, windowless building were a table of radios, a wall of maps, and the company commander, Capt. Robert Tilley. Tilley, a short, burr-headed muscular Marine, had the size and build of a middleweight fighter, and the temperament and reactions as well. Like many military men actively involved in the fighting, Captain Tilley was busy, shorthanded, and mistrustful of reporters. He came out slugging. "What do you want, another waste story?

"We had one reporter come out here to get a story, and we all helped him get his facts, and you know how he ended his story? 'What a waste.' That's all he had to say about the job these kids are doing. You know what's at stake here? Population and resource control. The VC are up in the Que Son Mountains. They come down into the lowlands to get rice and recruits. We keep them out.

"This is an infantry company," Captain Tilley asserted. "These men are all grunts. But they have an area of operation of forty square miles and they are responsible for the safety of over fifteen thousand civilians. We are also responsible for road security. Since last April there has been only one road-mine incident in our area. Do you think that's a waste?

"In the company area we have school for the PFs [Popular Forces that are combined with the Marines in the CUPP units]. We have two PFs from each platoon, and we have a Marine counterpart with each PF so they don't lose face by us having to teach them how to defend their village. If the Marines are going to school too, they don't mind. They come here for two days and two nights, they eat and sleep beside their Marine buddies, and we give them instruction in tactics, leadership, and marksmanship. At the end of the school we give them some extra gear as an incentive. Maybe a haversack or scout knife. Do you think that's a waste?

"We help them build schools. We run an experimental pig farm to improve their stock. Each platoon has a garden, and we're trying to get the Vietnamese to raise carrots, cabbage, beans, and watermelons to diversify their crops. We have introduced a species of fast-growing fish in the rice paddies to help them improve their diet. Our corpsmen deliver their babies and treat their kids. Do you think that's a waste?"

Captain Tilley was ready to slug it out, but I wasn't. Sergeant Merriman wanted to get the jeep back to Da Nang, as the roads were closed at dark and barbed-wire barricades set across them. To assist me at Baldy, the Marine PAO had provided Sgt. E. F. Burris. When the Army provided such men, they referred to them as "escorts." The Marines bristled at the word. They referred to Burris as my "bodyguard," and it was clear that was how Burris saw himself.

Burris wanted to get to the Third Platoon before dark. Burris and I were going to spend the night in the ville with CUPP 4. Captain Tilley shook my hand and with one shout had a driver and jeep at our service.

Protocol required a stop at the Third Platoon (Golf Three) Command Post, or C.P. We drove past the barbed wire and bunkers of Baldy and down a dusty gravel road. Rice paddies lined the road on each side, and beyond the paddies were treelines, or hedgerows, and low barren hills.

We came to a small ville at the side of the road. Immediately behind the ville was a steep-sided hill, and atop the hill was the Third Platoon C.P. The hill was encircled with barbed wire, and in the wire were booby traps, trip flares, and claymore mines. The hill was so steep it could not be reached by jeep, and all ammo, food, and water had to be carried by hand up a narrow trail through the barbed wire.

On top of the hill were fighting bunkers manned by Popular Forces, who lived in the ville below, and Peoples Self-Defense Forces (PSDFs). The PSDFs were boys and girls from the ville. They did not take part in operations but only in defense of the

C.P. and their homes. They were trained by the PFs and given discarded PF weapons. As the PFs were given discarded U.S. weapons, mostly World War II M-1s and carbines, the PSDFs were armed with the oldest and rustiest carbines.

In the center of the hill was the C.P., a two-level bunker with a radio and two beds — or racks, as the Marines called them — on the bottom level, which was dug into the rock of the hill, and sleeping quarters on the top level, which was sandbagged halfway up and enclosed with wire screen.

I stepped down into the entranceway, which was almost four feet lower than the top of the hill. "The only thing wrong with this bunker is that there's no way to get out of it if you're attacked," Lieutenant Smith said.

The space inside the command bunker was dark and close. Immediately inside the door was the ladder to the upper sleeping area. There the ceiling was low, and the floor was covered with racks except for a narrow space down the middle as a passageway. Underneath the racks was the Marines' personal gear —waterproof bags containing their extra clothing, shaving kits, pictures of their families, old letters, cigarettes, and a packet of stationery.

Paperback books lay about. Those on the floor or a rack belonged to whoever wanted to read them next. Those stuck under a bed, pillow, or poncho liner were private property until they were moved into the open. Spare boots and rain gear were also stored under the beds. Helmets, rifles, bandoleers of ammo, canteens, packs, gas masks, binoculars, flashlights, and cameras hung from the wall in confusion. The darkness, closeness, and clutter made the bunker look like a picture from the front during World War I.

Lieutenant Smith, the platoon leader, was a short, almost fat man with a smooth face, thin, short blond hair, and a small mouth that was quick to show displeasure. And Smith was usually displeased. Lieutenant Smith was a mustang—an officer who had come up through the ranks—and he was ill at ease with reporters and Annapolis graduates. He was a competent leader and combatant, but he did not like talking about national policy, MAC-V strategy, or company procedures. He was a doer, not a thinker, and sometimes the officer's insignia chafed.

Lieutenant Smith was not pleased to have two guests and was

insistent that we spend the night at the C.P. and that the platoon jeep be back inside the wire at Baldy before the gates were closed. "We'll get you down to CUPP 4 as soon as the road is cleared in the morning," he said. "We have some extra racks here. We bring the men one or two at a time to the C.P. for a day as a kind of platoon R and R. It gives them a chance to clean up and catch up on their sleep. The CUPP teams never come to the rear as a unit, and in the ville they never sleep more than two or three hours at a time."

Lieutenant Smith pointed me up the ladder into the sleeping quarters. "If we happen to get hit, just roll off on the floor, crawl over to the ladder, and drop down into the lower level. The roof won't take a direct mortar hit."

One man was already asleep. "That's Sergeant Waitulavich. Everyone calls him 'Rock' because that's what his name means in Lithuanian. He has more kills than anyone in the platoon." In his sleep, Sergeant Rock, young, blond, and athletic, looked more like a high school halfback than a professional Marine.

There was shouting outside, so the lieutenant and I climbed down the ladder and went out the door that was the single opening into the bunker. A couple of Marines labored up the hill with supplies. "We got the tube back," Staff Sergeant Shivers called. The C.P.'s 60mm mortar had been out of action for a couple of days and was being returned. Not only did the mortar provide protection for the C.P., but it was also used to provide support or illumination for the platoon's CUPP teams.

"We've got fifteen minutes before the truce starts," Lieutenant Smith said. I had forgotten it was Christmas Eve. "Set it up and let's get it registered. We'll let Charlie know we got it back." Lieutenant Smith took aim at a large rock just beyond the barbed wire of the hill and hit it with the third round.

It was cool and damp as darkness fell, and the trail through the barbed wire was closed. No one wanted to go into the cramped bunker, so they stood outside and watched the flares that bloomed over the rugged landscape. Barren hills covered with rocks and a few scrubby bushes were separated by small lush valleys of paddies and impenetrable treelines, or hedgerows.

Sergeant Shivers pointed out a stream that wound around the hills and explained how it could be dammed to conserve water for the rice fields and how it could also provide power for a sim-

ple waterwheel and grist mill. Shivers, a crusty former drill in-
structor, was a throwback to the "old Corps" with which I was
familiar, having served in the Marines during the Korean War.
Lean and mean, hard of eye, tough of mouth, Shivers spoke with
a voice that was difficult to argue with. "We're trying to suggest
a dam and a mill to the Vietnamese, but they have to feel it's
their idea. We'll help them build it, but if they think it's something we want, they won't work on it. It has to be something
they want."

Sergeant Burris, my escort, sat down and handed me a can of
rations. "We'll be going out to a CUPP team in the morning,"
he said. "I'll look after you, but try not to ask those guys for
things. I've been out in the field and had correspondents ask me
for my flak jacket, my food, my water, my cigarettes. It's hard
for those guys to get stuff out there."

In the distance was the hollow sound of rifle fire and the
muffled thump of grenades. "I was afraid of that," Lieutenant
Smith said. "They're hitting CUPP 4. Call them up and ask
what the hell is going on."

Everything was quiet at CUPP 4, but clearly visible from the
high ground of the C.P. were tracers arcing across the darkness
and then seeming to float into the night as they ricocheted. The
tracers were white. U.S. tracers were red, Communist tracers
white or green. "The VC must be having an intramural down
there," Lieutenant Smith said. "A couple of their units must have
bumped into each other and started shooting." The idea seemed
to make everyone happy.

After a couple of minutes, the firing abruptly stopped. Everyone waited for it to resume, but it did not. All was quiet except
for the thump of mortars, followed a few seconds later by the
pop of flares. "Time to open the presents," Lieutenant Smith
said, and when the men returned puzzled looks, he reminded
them, "It's Christmas Eve."

Except for one man on radio watch, everyone crowded into
the upper level of the bunker, where Lieutenant Smith had set
up a tree on an empty ammo case. A candle was lighted under
the tree—for illumination, not reverence. Around the tree were
packages which had been sent from groups in the States. Lieutenant Smith passed out the packages for his men to open. The
lieutenant handed me a package, but I declined the gift. I had

celebrated Christmas early, with my family before I left. And I didn't need the reassurance that these men sought, that back in the world somebody cared.

The packages contained playing cards, ballpoint pens (a treasure, as the moisture quickly ruined pens), candy, cakes, nuts, magazines, paperback books, games, stationery, instant fruitdrink mixes (also treasured because they masked the taste of halazone tablets in the water). The books, drink mixes, games, and eats were pooled to be shared by all. The pens and stationery were distributed.

Lieutenant Smith produced a bottle of bourbon from under his rack. Only a little was left, but he passed it around, and each man held the bottle against the candlelight to judge his fair share. After the bottle had passed around, Lieutenant Smith taking the last drink, the cards accompanying the packages were collected, and the wrapping and paper picked up to be burned.

Sergeant Rock took the cards from the packages. "I'll write and thank these people," he said. Lieutenant Smith gave him a box of stationery for the thank-you letters and an unopened package for the radio operator, who had missed the celebration. Those of us remaining on the upper level pulled off our boots and went to bed fully clothed.

I had not noticed the rats and mosquitoes until Lieutenant Smith blew out the light. In the darkness the mosquitoes buzzed, and the rats scurried over the roof and across the floor. The mosquitoes seemed immune to insect repellent, at least the repellent the government issued. The rats were enormous and reputedly ferocious when cornered. To the Vietnamese the rats were food. To the Americans the rats were a quick ticket home. Scuttlebutt was that a rat bite brought an immediate medevac and a seat on the Freedom Bird, the next plane out of Da Nang bound for home. It sounded tempting, but no one was eager for the series of rabies, plague, and tetanus shots that accompanied the plane ticket.

I slept lightly, somehow aware of the soft murmur of the PFs on watch, the hiss and crackle of the radio below, and the popping of flares. At midnight, Sergeant Rock yelled, and everybody got up to see the mortars at Baldy light up the sky with red, green, and white flares. It was Christmas Day. We watched as the mortars threw up a Christmas tree of dangling red and green flares with a white star at the top. Slowly the flares drifted to earth, and the night went black again. It was Christmas, but there was no peace, no joy, and nothing to do. After a moment of staring at the blackness, hoping for more, we stumbled back to bed.

Christmas Day dawned gray and damp as we waited for the road sweep to clear the way to CUPP 4. Two Marines carrying mine detectors came down the road, sweeping it for mines. They were backed up by a tank that rumbled along behind them.

By the time Burris and I got on the road, CUPP 4 had returned to their day position in the ville. CUPP 4, composed of a squad of Marines, a Navy corpsman, and approximately twenty-five Vietnamese Popular Forces, spent the night in one of several fixed night positions outside the ville. The night positions were nothing more than fighting holes, but by moving under cover of darkness, the Marines made it difficult for the VC to find them and pin them down, and by setting at least two ambushes, or Alley Cats, each night, they kept the VC out of the ville.

The PFs were the most poorly paid, poorly trained, poorly equipped forces in Vietnam. They were recruited to provide security for their own hamlet and could not be required to fight outside the district in which they lived. They were peasant farmers who lived with their families, farmed their land, and in their spare time learned military skills. Each day some of the PFs shared their hootches with the Marines, and each night some of them accompanied the Marines on patrols and ambushes. The PFs knew who belonged in the ville and who didn't, they knew the terrain and probable VC hiding places, and they were aware of any unusual or suspicious activity in the area.

The leader of CUPP 4 was twenty-year-old Cpl. Meddie Goyette, of Ithaca, New York. Corporal Goyette was in command of approximately forty men—about the same number of men commanded by most lieutenants. Although Goyette had no real authority over the PFs, who were commanded by a PF "honcho," he was their leader, and he was responsible for their conduct under fire. He was also reponsible for the safety of approximately one hundred families who lived in the ville.

I could not help being impressed by Corporal Goyette. Only weeks before, I had been teaching young men, Goyette's age and older, who did not want to be responsible for their girlfriends, their country's foreign policy, or their classroom attendance. More than one male student had told me, "You have to give me a passing grade. If I flunk out of school I'll be drafted and sent to Vietnam, and if I die it'll be your fault."

Responsibility did not seem to bother Goyette, who was blond with boyish good looks in the manner of Sergeant Rock. The two men bore a resemblance, although Rock was the older and heavier of the two, and Goyette the more laconic and laid-back.

The other Marines liked Goyette, trusted him, and liked being in the CUPP, although it meant they had no bunkers, no barbed wire, no regular bed, no showers, no movie, no mess hall, no NCO club, and no backup except for the guns of Baldy and a relief force of company size that could be quickly assembled at the combat base. None of the CUPP Marines I talked to believed a relief force would be allowed to leave Baldy after nightfall. "Too easy to ambush," they said.

In the villes they ate combat rations, carried their extra clothing and personal items on their backs, and their access to the PX was through the platoon jeep driver who came every day in a jeep and trailer bringing mail, ammo resupply, rations, and rumors.

"I was here from July 4 until December 9 before I even got to Baldy," said one Marine. In Da Nang, Baldy with its barren hills was the end of the world, but to the CUPP teams it was the symbol of civilization—showers (no hot water), mess hall, racks, PX, NCO club, and screened privies with a roof and a floor.

But the Marines liked the CUPP because, while the towns and villages of Vietnam were off-limits to most military personnel, the CUPP teams lived in the villes and got to know the people. "Some people spend their whole tour in Vietnam and never know a single Vietnamese. They can't tell a friend from an enemy. We know these people. We're part of their lives."

The Marines also liked the CUPP because they were on their own. Officers and staff NCOs were not often seen. Discipline was good—Goyette held rifle inspection once a week, and in spite of the primitive conditions, his men were clean shaven and closely cropped—but there was little military formality.

"Everyone knows what he is supposed to do, and he does it," Goyette said. He was an effective but unobtrusive leader, quiet to the point of reticence. When an ABC television crew came to do a story on CUPP 4, Goyette was cooperative but uncommunicative. He agreed to go through the motions of a patrol and an ambush for the camera, but it looked like what it was, and the crew left without a story.

The Marines of CUPP 4 were young, strikingly young, even with the background of young men in uniform, and they looked very tired. They had been awake most of the night because something or someone had set off a trip flare they had placed around their night position. The Marines and PFs responded by throwing fragmentation grenades. "We frag everything that moves at night," Goyette said. "At night a rifle will give away your position, but you can't tell where a frag comes from."

After throwing the grenades, they heard or saw nothing more, but they remained on the alert the rest of the night and returned to the ville as soon as it was light enough to see. "It makes for a long day," Goyette said, "but they go by fast out here. They all seem alike."

Once in the ville the PFs went to their homes, and the Marines scattered out in three hootches and began boiling water for coffee and the freeze-dried Long Range Patrol rations they called "long rats" but the Army called "lurps." Vietnamese children hung around to run errands, washing socks, filling canteens. The Marines passed out the unwanted portions of their rations. "I souvenir you this," they said, holding out packets of powdered milk, powdered coffee, sugar, chocolate — sometimes even Chiclets or candy.

Children in the ville were different from the children most servicemen and correspondents knew — the streetwise urchins of Saigon and Da Nang. I had been walking on Tu Do Street in Saigon when a boy, who looked two but was probably closer to six, caught my hand and walked with me. Like most Americans, I liked children, but when I looked down to smile at my new friend, I saw that while still gripping my hand, he had his thumb and finger in my pocket and was lifting my wallet.

One reporter I knew was approached by a group of smiling children who wanted him to take their picture. When they left, he discovered that his watch and wallet were gone.

In the villes, the CUPP Marines trusted the children to carry their personal belongings and even their rifles.

After eating, most of the Marines pulled off their wet boots and socks, laid them out to dry, and stretched out on the ground to rest. A few of them played with the children. "These kids are the only hope for this country," Goyette said. "The old people don't care. They just want to be left alone. If this country is ever going to have peace, it's up to these kids." All the children in the ville were friendly with the Marines. Some of them were suspected of giving information to the VC.

A villager came looking for Billy, a Vietnamese boy who acted as an unofficial interpreter. Most of the children in the ville had learned some English—usually the most expressive words—so that their usage was both comic and obscene.

"Fire in the hole," little boys shouted before throwing rocks. It was a cry the Marines used to warn of an imminent explosion, usually before throwing a grenade.

Billy was small with delicate features, and although he claimed to be sixteen years old, he looked several years younger than that. Goyette had promised Billy a rifle but had been unable to get one for him, so Billy accompanied the Marines on their operations carrying a grenade in each hand. He had no formal training but was able to communicate with the Marines, and he explained to Goyette that a hoi chanh (defector) had just given himself up to the village chief, who wanted Goyette to come and see.

Goyette and a couple of other Marines picked up their rifles, put on their helmets and flak jackets, and walked down the road to meet the hoi chanh, an elderly man who, according to Billy's translation, had been a rice commissar responsible for supplying rice to the VC. The man was a local villager, and his wife and children were clinging to him and weeping for joy at his return. The hoi chanh said that another man had tried to come with him, but when they had approached the Marines in their night position, they had been grenaded. His companion had been wounded and was now lying at the edge of the ville waiting for someone to come and get him.

The PF honcho dispatched some PFs to pick the man up, and Goyette radioed the platoon C.P. to report the hoi chanh. A jeep was sent to take the hoi chanh to Baldy for questioning, but first the village chief had to be reassured the man would be returned to the village. This required a great deal of explaining on the part of Goyette and Billy to the village chief, who clung to the hoi chanh along with the man's family.

"Tell the honcho they just want to question the hoi chanh for TT [short] time," Goyette said. "No one will hurt him."

After many pledges and tears the jeep left with the hoi chanh, the village chief left with the hoi chanh's family, and Goyette lay down to rest. An old papasan approached and began speaking to him. Goyette called Billy to find out what the man wanted, and Billy explained that the man's family was having a feast on the anniversary of the death of a family member and that Goyette was invited. Goyette accepted reluctantly. As I was the oldest American in the ville and had been introduced as a visiting honcho, I was also invited to come. Acceptance meant that Sergeant Burris would also have to go, but not to accept would have been an insult.

Goyette picked up his flak jacket and rifle and told the other members of the squad where we were going. Although the ville was small and considered "friendly," it was widely scattered with only a few hootches on either side of the road to Baldy. The others were spread out along ditches and treelines, which permitted infiltration. Two days earlier four PFs had been ambushed on the edge of the ville. One of them was killed. The others dropped behind a paddy dike and were rescued by their Marine and PF buddies, who came running at the first sound of gunfire.

"We've got good PFs," Goyette said. "They'll stand and fight. They won't run." He was also careful to take his rifle wherever he went.

As we walked along the footpath to the house, Goyette and Billy explained the rules of etiquette. We should not sit with our feet pointed at anyone. We should not touch anyone, even children, and we especially should not pat them on the head. The name of the deceased must not be spoken. The family celebrating the anniversary feast would offer the best food they had, and we should not pretend that what the Marines ate was better. To eat lightly as though we regarded the family too poor to feed us properly would be an insult. When we were full, we should leave something in our cup or bowl, as an empty bowl would indicate we were still hungry and we would be given more.

The house consisted of two separate buildings—one composed of a single room with a plank bed, and the other more than twice as large with a flimsy partition. Both of the buildings were typical low-roofed thatch houses built on bamboo frames. The two buildings were joined by a flagstone patio which was used for drying rice, and a masonry wall ran along one side of the patio parallel with the road to Baldy. Along one side of the house was a brushy drainage ditch. Goyette and Burris regarded the ditch with suspicion.

We were greeted ceremoniously by our host—the oldest male presided—who was saying his prayers at an outside altar. One member of the household asked through Billy that rifles not be brought near the altar. Goyette and Burris put their rifles and flak jackets against the masonry wall, close enough to be watched. Suddenly a heavy rain fell, and we were ushered into the smaller of the two buildings. As there were no doors or windows, one wall was removed for light and access. The altar was carried into the small building, and a table was set before the altar. Billy got Goyette's and Burris's rifles and placed them out of the rain.

While the papasan lighted joss sticks and continued his prayers, we were invited to sit on benches along either side of the table. There was some maneuvering, as none of the Americans wanted to sit with his back to the ditch. Goyette, Burris, and I sat on one side, and the bench promptly collapsed under our weight, as each of us outweighed the average Vietnamese male by fifty pounds. With a great deal of embarrassed bowing and apologizing, our broken bench was exchanged for the other bench. Several of the Vietnamese men pressed on the bench to demonstrate its strength, but Goyette decided he and Burris would sit with their backs to the ditch but close to the rifles, and Billy and I would sit on the opposite side. A plank bed, consisting of a sheet of plywood over a wooden frame, was pulled near the table, and Billy and I sat on it. The other male guests took whatever space was left.

Women came from the larger house bringing bottles of banana rum. After placing ritual offerings of food on the altar, the old papasan poured the sweetish oily drink into C-ration cans that had the lids bent back for handles. After the cans had been passed around, we all drank with much nodding of the head in appreciation. "Number one," the Americans said, and the Vietnamese agreed as the papasan refilled the cups.

While the women brought bowls of noodles, rice, and meat and a wine bottle filled with nuoc mam, the papasan passed out chopsticks, after first wiping them with his fingers. The chopsticks were peeled branches from the trees in the ditch, and their crudity should not have surprised me but did. Being a squeamish American accustomed to antiseptic kitchens and service, I was dismayed that the chopsticks were not new but had been discolored from age and polished from use.

Goyette identified the slivers of boiled duck, bite-size fish with their heads intact, and a delicacy of pork fat pressed with congealed pig's blood. I ate slowly, pretending awkwardness with the chopsticks as an excuse for not eating more. The subterfuge failed. The hospitable Vietnamese beside me, who was missing both his upper and lower front teeth, noticed my difficulty and, after carefully licking his chopsticks, assisted me, first by putting food in my bowl of noodles, and then by placing selected delicacies in my mouth.

Women came from the big house proudly bearing bowls of molded rice. The papasan picked up some with his chopsticks and tasted it. "Number one," he said, picking up more and placing it first in Goyette's mouth and then in mine. "Number one," the other guests echoed, helping themselves. Goyette explained that the rice cake was the number one of all the number one dishes. "Number one," we agreed.

Billy, who was aggressively outgoing with the Marines, appeared shy and awkward with the Vietnamese. He was the only young person at the table other than the Marines. He was sitting with older, venerable men, and he was aware of the impropriety. He did not look up, and he spoke only when Goyette asked him to explain that we were full.

The other guests seemed disappointed when the papasan called for tea, and they quickly began emptying their bowls. The women came bringing tea in rusting C-ration cans. With the women came children, who hung around the table looking at the food. They would get what the men left. Goyette passed out Salems, and the men smoked as they finished their tea. Mentholated Salems were the favorite cigarettes of the Vietnamese.

After the tea and cigarettes we excused ourselves and left. The rain had stopped, and the sun was shining. Four Marines were waiting nearby. Although I had not noticed them, they had drifted down to our end of the ville to provide security. With Goyette they studied the brushy ditch. Under the trees was the ruins of a VC bunker. Goyette set the Marines to clearing the brush from the ditch with crude Vietnamese sickles while he studied the masonry wall beside the hootch where we had just eaten. "If we take fire from that wall, we'll have to put a LAW through it," Goyette said. A LAW was a one-shot disposable bazooka for use against armor and fortified positions. Two weeks later the VC slipped down the ditch and threw Chicom grenades at the Marines, and the wall was blown away.

Abruptly the rain began falling again, and the Marines abandoned the clearing for a while and headed for the hootches. Burris and I ran into a hootch and sat down on the pounded-earth floor. The earth floor had been raised several inches above ground level but nevertheless stayed damp during the rainy season and smelled of urine. There was no one in the hootch and no furniture except for a plank bed and hammock. Along one side of the hootch was a pig sty containing two of the typical swaybacked pigs. I tried leaning against a wall, but it was not strong enough to support me.

After a few minutes the rain stopped, and I went outside to discover that while we had been at dinner, a new man had come to the ville. He was Cpl. Wayne Hill of Burlington, Iowa, and he had a dog with him. Ricochet, a large mixed-breed German shepherd, was specially trained to detect buried mines and booby traps. Like most of the American dogs, Ricochet did not like Vietnamese, and Corporal Hill kept him out of the hootches and under a cover. The cover was for protection not from the rain but from the sun.

"The heat really kicks the dog's ass," said Hill, who not only was bigger but had more hair than any Marine in the ville. In contrast to the CUPP Marines, Hill looked like he ate and slept well. "When we're out in the field, I have to carry twenty-two canteens of water for me and the dog, plus food for both of us. But you don't feed them much. That's the way they train them. They work for food. You got to keep them hungry."

Ricochet was thin and had a mean, hungry look about him which might have been the reason the PFs kept their distance from the dog, but Hill had to warn the children to stay away. The children were fascinated by the dog, not only because Ric was so much larger than Vietnamese dogs but also because Hill could make the dog do tricks.

"It costs sixteen thousand dollars to train one of these dogs," said Hill, taking Ric off the leash and directing him with hand signals to sit, lie, stay, come—not for the benefit of the children or the Marines who watched, but to keep the dog in training. "They are trained for eighteen weeks back in the world, then we are trained with them for six weeks in Okinawa. After ten days in the field, we take them back to the rear and retrain them for three days to keep them sharp. Some of these guys think that's pretty soft spending only ten days at a time out here, but for those ten days I'm walking point."

After working the dog, Hill wrestled with him for a while. "You get real tight with these dogs," Hill said. "I'm going to try to buy Ric when I go back to the world. I heard you could do that. He'll have to be quarantined in Okinawa for a while, but I don't care. If I leave him here the Vietnamese will eat him."

The sky seemed to be clearing, so the Marines peeled off their wet shirts and socks. Those who had been clearing the ditch went back for another try. A couple of Marines inspected the PFs' rifles, cleaning those that needed it, and another party went out to work in the team's garden.

On land that had been donated by the ville, the Marines had planted carrots, lettuce, cabbage, beets, beans, and watermelons. They worked with the Vietnamese to show them how the crops were best raised, without implying that they knew more than the Vietnamese, who had been farming all their lives. "It's tricky," said Goyette, who had done no farming in Ithaca, New York. "They've never seen some of these things before, but if you act like you know something they don't, they lose face and won't work anymore."

No one was sure what the reaction would be when the Vietnamese tasted the vegetables for the first time, but already they had had to fence out the water buffalo that took a liking to the garden. The only barbed wire in the ville protected the garden from the buffalo.

Two girls came down the road on bicycles with bags of soft drinks and beer hanging from the handlebars. The Marines interrupted their chores to flirt with the girls and buy the lukewarm soft drinks, which sold for about fifty cents. Warm beer was ninety cents. "Hell, we don't have anything else to spend money on," said one Marine.

The girls' conversation with the Marines was composed of equal parts of Vietnamese slang, mispronounced French, pidgin English, and GI obscenity.

"Let me have a Pepsi," said one Marine. "I'll pay you later."

"No bit," the girl said. (I don't understand.)

"You bit," the Marine said. "TT money." TT was used by the Marines for any diminutive from *few* to *small*.

"You boo coo money," the girl said. "You Cheap Charlie." Nevertheless she handed him a can of Sprite.

"Pepsi," he said. "No Sprite."

"Number one," she said. "You dien cai dau." (Crazy.)

"You dinky dow. Sprite number ten. Pepsi Cola."

The other girl pretended she was going to leave without returning change. "I di-di," she said.

"You di-di, you cacadow," a Marine answered. (You go, you die.)

I tried to take a picture of the girls, but they agreed only after persuasion. The girls feared that if I took a photograph, I would capture their spirit in the picture. "If you hang on the wall, maybe OK," she said. "But if you shitcan (throw away), maybe I die."

On their bicycles the soda girls were the most mobile Vietnamese in the area. Going up and down the roads and through the villes, they saw and heard many things that were useful to the Marines. One of the girls regularly told the Marines of VC movement. Because of this she had been shot at several times by snipers along the road. She frequently changed her appearance and seldom slept in the same place twice.

After the girls left, the Marines roughhoused with the kids and PFs and played football in the road with a tin can until the platoon driver came out with mail and hot food. The company tried to get one hot meal to the CUPP teams every day. The men lined up around the trailer and picked up a paper plate which they loaded with roast beef, mashed potatoes, gravy, salad, and cups of ice cream.

"Here comes the nook," someone said as heavy rain fell again. The line around the trailer moved a little faster as the men filled their plates and moved into the closest hootch before the mashed potatoes ran, the ice cream melted, and the plates collapsed in the rain.

"There's too many people in here," Goyette said as I sat on the floor to eat. "One RPG (Rocket-Propelled Grenade) would wipe out everybody." Some of the men put on their rain gear and stood in the rain to eat. After a few minutes the torrent stopped, and everyone moved outside.

The jeep driver left behind extra ice cream, cans of nuts, and inexpensive gifts, which were passed out to the children. He also left the team's share of the Christmas packages from the States. The men opened the packages, shouting to call attention to anything that was amusing, interesting, or noteworthy. Religious periodicals were unceremoniously disposed of. Other magazines and books were passed around. They were something else to carry around by men who had little time to read in the daytime and no way to read at night. Most of them were discarded. Pens and stationery were the only presents that everyone claimed.

One of the packages contained the photograph of a plain-faced girl with her name and address on the back. The photograph was passed around and objectively appraised. "Her nose is too thin." "Yeah, but look at those tits." One of the Marines declared his intention to write the girl, who was from the same state, and the photograph was given to him. "Maybe I'll go see her when I go back to the world," he said.

Those who had gotten mail had been reading it at every opportunity, and once the distraction of the photograph was over, they returned to it again. "Hey, you got two letters," said one Marine to his buddy.

"One from my girlfriend and one from my mother."

"Let me read one of them, I didn't get any."

Obligingly, the buddy handed over the unopened letter from his mother.

A red painted helicopter swung low over the ville, and a man in a Santa Claus suit waved from the door. "That's Bob Hope," someone yelled. He was drowned out in a chorus of profanity. "Bob Hope is not coming out here to entertain fourteen guys." There was some speculation as to who the Santa Claus was, and the general opinion was that it was the Old Man, Captain Tilley. "You wouldn't catch me hanging out the door of a helicopter flying that low around here," said one Marine. It proved to be a unanimous opinion.

Goyette, who had been called to the radio, returned to say that there would be only one patrol that day, as an operation was planned that night. The Marines crowded around asking for more information, which Goyette did not have. "Lieutenant Smith is coming out to brief us," he said.

"What's today?" Corporal Payne asked.

"The twenty-fifth," someone answered, after consulting his watch.

For a few seconds no one spoke, and then Corporal Payne said, "It's Christmas Day, you dumbass. Why do you think they sent out all that food?"

Suddenly the Marines began to roughhouse, trying to throw each other to the ground and demonstrating what they were going to do to the VC. "There are only two days that mean anything out here," Payne explained. "The day you go on R and R, and the day you go home."

Goyette watched the men as they scuffled and pretended to shoot and stab each other. "That's why they call us 'gungy Golf,'" he said. "When those PFs were ambushed, these guys went charging across the rice paddies in their shorts. Some of them didn't even put their boots on. Last month we had more kills and captures than any company in Vietnam. And we're supposed to be a pacification company."

Turning to the men, Goyette said, "Who's going on the patrol?" Without a word several of the Marines picked up their flak jackets and rifles. Goyette took down their names and zap numbers and discussed the route they were going to take. The patrol was to check for strange faces in the ville or for unusual activity along the footpaths. Hill offered to take his dog, but Goyette felt there was little likelihood of mines or booby traps in the ville. The PF honcho assigned some PFs to go along, and the men strung out as they walked across the road, taking their positions in the patrol.

The ville was not a formal unit like an American town with streets and boundaries but was spread over the landscape. Even those houses located close together were separated from each other by trees and clumps of bushes so that it was impossible to stand at any place in the ville and see more than two or three hootches. Other hootches were separated by rice fields, the low-roofed buildings almost hidden by treelines or bamboo thickets.

The patrol moved slowly down the slippery footpaths through the ville, stopping frequently to look in the open houses, checking the trails for signs of heavy movement. Theoretically there was a truce on, but no one believed it. The Marines were silent, alert, but not tense. The PFs strolled along, singing as they went. The PFs did not accompany the Marines just for the training; they knew who belonged in the ville, and they were the first to recognize something foreign or suspicious.

The patrol worked through the most heavily populated part of the ville and then began walking across narrow paddy dikes and along treelines to check on the more remote houses. The patrol slowed. "That's where the PFs were ambushed two days ago," Corporal Payne said, pointing out the paddy dike behind which they had taken cover. Everything seemed serene. The rice fields were empty. Not a leaf rustled in the treelines. Rain fell again, and the patrol moved a little faster as the PFs began taking shortcuts and getting ahead. "They don't like rain," Payne said.

To Payne the rain seemed just another nuisance in a year when only hazard counted.

When the patrol reached the farthest house in the ville and checked the footpaths around it, they headed back toward the road. When they reached the road at the outskirts of the ville, the patrol was over. The PFs struck out separately for their homes. The Marines slung their rifles and began straggling. "That's the way it is 90 percent of the time," Payne said. "Nothing." He sounded disappointed.

At the edge of the ville was a new concrete building. "That's the school," Payne said. "They wanted a school, so we helped them build it. We even supplied the material, a bag of cement at a time to eliminate graft. We helped them build that bridge over the stream too so they can get to the market. They figure we built the bridge for ourselves, since we use it too, and they won't defend it. But they'll defend the school. They haven't been able to get a teacher though."

In the struggle for the peasants' minds, the schools were a major VC target. The Viet Cong proudly publicized the fact that in the hamlets they controlled there were schools for everyone. The government of South Vietnam, belatedly and with U.S. support, also tried to provide schools, but the schools had to be constantly guarded against the VC, who burned the buildings and assassinated or terrorized the teachers. No teacher would come to the ville until he was certain he was safe from Viet Cong terror.

Farther down the road was a metal drum supported by bamboo poles. "That's the village shower," Payne said. "All you have to do is get someone to pour water in the top while you stand under it. Before we put that up, the only way we had to take baths was to throw buckets of cold water at each other."

As the patrol neared the day position, Lieutenant Smith and Staff Sergeant Shivers drove up in the jeep. As the men gathered around the jeep, so did the children, and Lieutenant Smith shooed them away. Like most mustangs he was impatient with words and distrustful of elaborate plans.

"You'll leave here at 2200. There will be two KTs. Goyette will lead one, Sergeant Rock will take the other. That will leave four Marines and a handful of PFs with your gear. You'll link up with the C.P. group at the old trailroad track. We'll move into position and sweep the villes at 0300. After that we'll wait for daylight and sweep through the area. We've never followed a night op with a day sweep, so we'll catch them by surprise. Any questions?"

The Marines had none, but I did. "What are KTs?"

"We don't call them that any more," Lieutenant Smith said. "We just call them teams. There will be two teams."

"What are KTs?" I whispered to Goyette.

"Killer teams. We don't call them that any more," he said. "The papers wrote a lot of bad stuff about it, so we had to change the name."

"Remember your rules of conduct of fire," Lieutenant Smith was saying. "You can't shoot a man unless he is carrying a rifle or a pack or unless he shoots at you."

The rules of conduct of fire were intended to reduce civilian casualties and to soften public opinion back home, where people didn't have to stalk through dense jungles or pitch-black villes waiting for the enemy to fire first. These Marines cared little about public relations and openly grumbled about rules they considered not only unfair and one-sided but dangerous to their lives. "It's unrealistic," one of them said. "It's stupid. If you see a guy carrying a grenade, you can't shoot him unless he throws it at you."

While Lieutenant Smith went over details with Corporal Goyette and the PF honcho, Sergeant Shivers took the other Marines aside. Shivers was not many years older than the other

Marines, but he was of a different generation. The "new breed" Marines like Rock and Goyette were perhaps as tough and professional, as clean shaven and disciplined, but they were more relaxed about it. To Shivers, the Corps was not a career, it was a religion, and Shivers was not only priest but inquisitor.

"Pick you out a PF you trust, and tell him he is to stay with you," Shivers told them. "Tell him he is to go down when you go down. He is to get up when you get up. He is to move when you move, and he is not to fire until you fire. Remember at night to shoot low. A ricochet will kill a man just as well as a direct hit. You're going to get excited when the shooting starts, so just remember what you've been taught. Do the job you were trained to do."

Shivers eyed the men, sniffing the air for heretical attitudes. "I'm going to make a prediction," he said. "I predict that tomorrow some of you fuckers are going to die."

He tried to stare the men down, and when he failed, he wished them good luck and walked away.

For a few minutes there was the confusion of a schoolyard ball game as the Marines and PFs went around picking out buddies. "You're going with me, OK?" "You stick with me." "I'm taking Jack Benny," shouted one Marine, referring to a PF who not only looked like Jack Benny but walked like him as well. Some of the PFs picked the Marines they wanted to accompany them.

Having planned their evening and next day, some of the men approached the jeep driver with shopping requests. Goyette wanted a machete to cut brush from the ditch. The others wanted socks, towels, toothpaste. "You can get to the PX, and we can't," they said.

"I don't have time for that," the jeep driver said. "I'm driving for the whole platoon."

"We have time to check that bridge you drive over every day," Goyette said pointedly.

The argument ended with the jeep driver taking the orders but refusing to say when he would fill them.

After they had drifted away, the jeep driver turned to me for sympathy. "They think I've got a slide because I sleep behind the wire at Baldy, but they don't realize I'm out here on these roads alone. If they get hit, they die with their friends beside them. If a sniper gets me or the jeep hits a mine, I die alone. The best

I can hope is that I die quick and don't have to lay out there waiting for Charlie to come finish me."

When the dog handler, Hill, found that CUPP 4 would make up two teams for the operation, leaving only four Marines and the other PFs to protect the gear and the ville, he wanted the jeep driver to take the dog to Baldy. "I'm afraid to leave him here with just four Marines. These dogs are valuable. The VC have a price on them."

Shivers wanted the dog to go on the operation. "I'll leave the dog and go on the op, or I'll bring the dog out in the morning," Hill said, "but the dogs just aren't any good at night, and they're hard to handle. Ric's not a scout dog, and if he sees something you can't keep him quiet."

After some discussion it was decided that the dog would go to Baldy, where he would be safe. Hill would stay behind to help guard the gear and the ville and would pick up the dog at daylight and join the operation.

It made little difference to the Marines who went and who stayed behind, as staying behind in such a small force was at least as dangerous as going on the operation. Since the machine gunner was suffering from unhealed shrapnel wounds in the legs which he was supposed to keep dry, Goyette asked him to stay behind. It was as impossible to keep the wounds dry in the ville as it was in the bush, but Goyette wanted to save him from the humping the teams would have to do.

Goyette asked for volunteers to go with Rock. There was some reluctance at first, not because of dislike for Waitulavich, but because he was considered to be the gungiest Marine in the platoon, and no one wanted to appear to be anxious to go with him, or disloyal to Goyette. After the first volunteer, a pimple-faced PFC wearing glasses, others also volunteered quickly but diffidently. "OK, I'll go," they said, and most of them said it without looking at anyone.

"One other thing," said Lieutenant Smith. "We found a booby trap made of a 105 round near the C.P." There were low whistles. A 105 had a kill radius of up to 175 meters. The booby trap had been discovered and reported by a child, who had been rewarded under the Voluntary Informant Program. Payment for a booby trap that had been set and placed ranged from twenty-five hundred to ten thousand piasters, about ten to forty dollars.

"Keep your eyes open," Lieutenant Smith said. "And tell the kids you'll pay them for any booby traps they report. Tell them not to mess with them, just report them."

Lieutenant Smith asked me to return to the C.P. with him. I didn't want to, because I had spent the day with CUPP 4 and was getting some idea of what their routine was like. Also, I was an outsider who had come to evaluate those men by some standard, some code of morality and bravery of my own making. It was not an unfamiliar experience to me. In the classroom I sat on the other side of the desk, and no matter how close I got to students or how much they liked me, I stood in judgment on them. Nevertheless, the students knew that in the dim-distant past, I had sat where they were sitting and knew something of their lot and therefore had some basis on which to evaluate them fairly. I didn't want to evaluate CUPP 4 from the relative comfort and safety of the platoon C.P.

Lieutenant Smith pointed out that I would not be with CUPP 4 during the operation. During the operation, the only way I would know what was going on was to be with the C.P. group, the communication center of the operation. I agreed to return to the C.P.

Lieutenant Smith made certain that CUPP 4 had all the ammunition and supplies it needed, then he and Sergeant Shivers returned to the C.P., taking Sergeant Burris and me with them. Sergeant Rock, who was at the C.P., was to join CUPP 4 before darkness closed the road.

There were some new faces at the Third Platoon C.P. Lieutenant McCay, an artillery officer, was going on the operation to direct artillery fire support. Also, McCay wanted to season his radio operator, Private First Class Hernandez, who was lacking in combat experience. Lieutenant Fred McDonnell was going to replace Lieutenant Smith as platoon leader, and he wanted to observe the platoon in the field and get to know the men before he took command. Lieutenant Smith, who was an experienced combat officer with a reputation as a tireless if impatient leader, was going to take over Second Platoon, which had a larger area of operation and was currently making more contact with the enemy.

Lieutenants McCay and McDonnell appeared smooth and

fresh compared with Smith, who looked more like a rumpled war-horse. They seemed scarcely older than Goyette, but they were college men, officers and gentlemen, with handsome faces, neat camouflage uniforms, and soft voices. McCay wore glasses as became a studious artillery officer, and McDonnell spoke in commanding but nasal tones.

When the conversation turned to college, football games, and fraternities, Lieutenant Smith was ill at ease. Although he was the more experienced officer, Smith seemed acutely aware of the humble path he had taken to his present position. When the war was over and the demand for second lieutenants ended, Smith would return to the ranks, McCay and McDonnell would not. When his enlistment was up, Smith would reenlist, McCay and McDonnell would not. The three officers held the same rank, but none of them saw it that way. Smith envied their polish and assumption. They envied his experience.

Lieutenant Smith looked at his watch. "Truce is over," he said as darkness fell quickly under heavy skies. Already the mortars at Baldy were popping flares over the countryside. Shivers checked to see that the gates in the barbed wire were closed, and then he took a look in the PF and PSDF bunkers.

In contrast to the command bunker, the PF bunkers were extremely bare. A couple of them had rough plank beds; the others contained nothing except boxes of hand flares (or "pop-ups"), grenades, and the "hell boxes" that triggered the claymores on the slopes below. The PFs talked quietly in the light of candles made of the waxed C-ration cartons.

Before returning to the command bunker, Shivers climbed atop it and took a long look at the countryside through the starlight scope, or "green eye," that used the light of the stars to enable a man to see in the darkness. I followed him up for a look. Through the scope everything appeared in shades of green, but I could detect people moving about in the ville a hundred or so meters away, people who must have been certain their actions were hidden by the mantle of darkness. "Do the VC have these things?" I asked, wondering if I might not at that very moment be under observation by some VC sniper.

"We've captured some of theirs," Shivers said, "but they're not as good as ours. Are you going to write one of those 'How I zapped the Cong and found God' stories?"

"What's that?"

"You know. A guy comes out here for a couple of days and writes about how smart he is and how he would fight the war and how painful the war is to him." Shivers had picked up four "purple hurts" for wounds received during his tours of duty in Vietnam.

A lot of men, many of them not journalists, some not writers of any kind, visited Vietnam for a few days, weeks, or months; sampled the prostitutes, the drugs, the violence; and then wrote confessional pieces about the suffering of their consciences or body or soul. Many, including myself, did not have the expertise to see the war in a global or international perspective, or the fighting in a strategic or tactical context. We tended to view the war in terms of the corruption of the men who did or didn't fight and the suffering in terms of the women and children caught in the crossfire. Our story was how Phu Bai smelled, and Tu Do repelled, and MAC-V lied.

Sergeant Shivers's question was a tough one for me to answer because I was a novelist and a college professor with no knowledge of Vietnamese history and culture, international politics and treaties, or the national intent of any of the countries involved. I was looking for stories of how men did their jobs under difficult, even dangerous situations, and all I had to bring to the stories was my experience as a man and sensibility as a writer. I admitted I was after the kind of story Sergeant Shivers referred to, but I wanted to write about him and the others, not about how my soul was or was not edified by sharing a few hours and days of their months and years.

When we climbed down off the bunker, the Marines were lined up before the command bunker. "I want everyone to blacken their faces," Lieutenant Smith said. "I don't want anyone's face shining."

After blacking our faces with grease paint, Shivers and I went into the lower level of the bunker and sat on the racks. The only light was from the Coleman lantern over the radio. Shivers got out his "grease gun," a .45-caliber submachine gun carried by tank crews in World War II, and began taping two ammo magazines together. The magazines were reversed, so that when one was empty, he could remove it, turn it over, and have a full magazine ready.

"I thought you weren't going," said Lieutenant Smith, who stood in the entrance.

"Well, I always say I'm not, and then I get to thinking, 'What if something happened and I missed it?'" Smith looked at him, considering whether or not to discourage him. "One more purple hurt and they have to send me home," Shivers said.

Lieutenant Smith broke open a box and handed me a battle dressing. "Carry it in your right trouser pocket so the corpsman will know where to look," he said. "Do you want a rifle?"

"I'm a noncombatant," I said, a bit startled. The Army had not offered me a weapon; the Army had informed me that I was not to carry one. I showed Lieutenant Smith the noncombatant I.D. card I had gotten at JUSPAO, the Joint U.S. Public Affairs Office in Saigon. I had been given two cards, one to keep on my person at all times, and one to hand over in the event I was captured.

"Do you think Charlie will be able to see that in the dark?" Smith asked.

I had thought of that, of course. The card was of wallet size and of no use unless I was captured. How to stay alive long enough to be captured was left to the initiative of the individual. A few correspondents had been captured; many more had died in combat areas and situations. Nevertheless, many correspondents refused to carry a weapon, believing that to do so not only marked them as a combatant but marked all correspondents as combatants or potentially combatants, adding peril to the danger they were voluntarily facing.

That view was an important consideration. Nevertheless, the enemy gave little evidence of knowing a combatant from a noncombatant, or of caring which was which, but if they had cared and had been able to tell, most weapons were not selective. Bombs, mines, and booby traps had no eyes, and most bullets were aimed at areas and points rather than individual targets.

Some correspondents did carry weapons in combat areas, particularly when they were with small units that could not provide much safety or promise speedy evacuation in dangerous situations. I was going to be with a small unit; nevertheless, I declined the weapon. "I've got a bodyguard," I said, indicating Sergeant Burris, even though I knew that Burris would prefer that I carry a weapon and cover my own ass.

The reason I declined a weapon was not for humanitarian or

ethical considerations but because I wanted to avoid the responsibility that went with it. I didn't want my life to depend on my skill and ability to make decisions under fire. I didn't want to come upon a stranger suddenly and have to decide in a split second whether it was a man, woman, or child that confronted me and whether that person constituted a threat to my life. And I didn't want to have to spend the rest of my life as a man who had accidentally, though intentionally, killed a civilian, or as a man bereft of a limb or eyesight or with the knowledge that someone else had died because I was unable to kill without hesitation.

It was very quiet in the lower level of the bunker. A few men smoked or dozed. I suffered some remorse for putting Sergeant Burris in a position where he might have to risk his life to save mine. Outside, the PFs were talking or softly singing and flares were popping, but inside there was only the crackle of the radio and the hiss of the lantern.

"There are some racks topside if anyone wants to sleep," Smith said. Thinking how arduous the next day might be, I considered stretching out on a rack, although I knew I wouldn't be able to sleep.

Suddenly the radio came to life. "Be advised CUPP 4 has taken mortar rounds and a light probe," Corporal Goyette reported.

Everyone rushed out of the bunker for a look, although nothing could be seen but a few ricochets floating high in the air. "They're running out of pop-ups," the radio operator yelled. "They want some illum."

"Break out some flares," Lieutenant Smith said, adjusting the mortar.

Shivers ripped the lid off a box, pulled the pin on a flare, and yelled, "Fire in the hole," before dropping it in the tube.

"On the way," Smith called. "Tell them to adjust."

In a few seconds the flare popped and swung slowly from its parachute. "Add one hundred," the operator called.

Smith adjusted, and Shivers dropped another flare into the tube. "On target," the operator called. "Keep them coming."

"Call up arty [artillery] and let them fire the illum," Smith said to McCay.

Lieutenant McCay, who had his map in hand and his radioman standing by him, called the battery at Baldy and gave them the grid coordinates. In a couple of minutes they had taken over the task of providing illumination for CUPP 4.

"They've beaten them off," the radio operator called. "Charlie di-died."

"Keep the illum going anyway," Smith said. "Find out which way they pulled back, and see if there are any casualties."

"One man has a TT head wound. He wouldn't have that if he had been wearing a helmet. They think the gooks are going down the railroad track."

"That's the way we're going," Shivers said. The VC had taken the same path the operation was going to take.

"See if we can get some arty in there before they get away."

McCay called arty again giving them the coordinates, but artillery couldn't get a clearance to fire because of a "friendly overlay." Civilian habitations and positions of friendly troops were marked on the map. According to the map, there was a ville at the coordinates McCay had called in—and perhaps there once had been such a ville, but no one in Third Platoon had ever seen it or any remains of it.

"Hell, there's nothing in there but CUPP 4," Lieutenant Smith said. One of the continuing frustrations was the inability to get artillery quickly on available targets. Or to get artillery at all. Every CUPP team had stories of being pinned down by enemy fire and unable to get artillery support because the fire was coming from a "friendly overlay."

Lieutenant Smith decided to interdict the area with his own mortar. He pointed out the target, which was over an intervening hill. McCay estimated the range, adjusted the mortar, and fired a flare. The first flare descended on top of the hill. The second flare burned for a moment and then dropped on the other side of the hill. "That's it, drop some high explosive on them," said Lieutenant Smith, and Lieutenant McCay dropped three rounds behind the hill. "At least they won't be waiting for us when we go down the railroad track," Smith said.

We stood around waiting for something else to happen but nothing did. The whole thing had taken only a few minutes and had ended as abruptly as it had begun, without resolution or even relief because it might occur again in a few minutes.

"Those CUPP teams can be overrun any time Charlies wants to pay the price," Lieutenant Smith said. "The only thing they've got going for them is that they move several times every night, and Charlie doesn't know where they are. That's the reason I wanted you with the C.P. group."

I should have felt relief, but what I felt was disappointment, and a little bit of guilt. I had spent the day with them and then returned to the C.P. The feeling was akin to attending practice and missing the game. It wasn't the danger that I imagined I had missed, it was the being there, the sharing of danger. I was quickly to learn that CUPP 4 had none of those feelings. The incident was routine, almost a nightly occurrence.

After a time we all went back inside and sat down. Lieutenant Smith was clearly troubled. "This operation is going to leave CUPP 4 with just four Marines and a handful of PFs all night, and Charlie already knows their position." No one spoke as Smith worked on the problem. "I can't leave CUPP 4 with just four men to defend the ville. We're going to have to call off the night part of the operation. Call up the teams and tell them we'll move out of here at 0430, and get in position before daylight to go through the sweep as planned," he said to the radio operator. He looked around for signs of disapproval.

"That's the only thing to do," Shivers said.

"Well, we might as well see if we can get some sleep. There's racks topside," Smith said.

We went to sleep fully clothed with our helmets, flak jackets, and canteens close at hand so we could find them in the dark. When I was awakened it was pitch black inside the bunker, but I picked up my gear by feel and followed the others down the ladder. Outside it was scarcely lighter than inside, and the air was damp and chill. Shivers took a look around with the star scope for a possible ambush, and then we stumbled down the steep path with the PFs closing the barbed wire behind us. At the bottom of the hill was the PF honcho with several PFs. There was a quick check of personnel, and then silently two files were formed, and we began marching down the road that had not yet been swept for mines.

We were warned to watch for mines, but the warning was useless in the darkness. I tried not to think about the 105 round that had been found nearby or to remember that 60 percent of all casualties in Vietnam were caused by booby traps and mines or that most such wounds resulted in the loss of one or more limbs. We had been told to keep a proper interval so that one mine wouldn't hit several people, but I found it impossible to keep any kind of interval and see the man ahead. It was so dark I found it difficult just to stay on the road, and the blackness of the rice paddies could have concealed the entire army of North Vietnam.

The line moved in fits and starts, and I bumped into the man ahead of me, who turned and without a sound let me know that he did not want me walking on his back or triggering a mine that would kill him as well as me.

The air was so damp it was difficult to know precisely when it became a fine mist that covered my helmet and jacket with a layer of dew. I zipped my flak jacket over my camera, hoping to keep it dry. Still we plodded forward, and I found myself looking over my shoulder for reassurance that a VC battalion had not infiltrated the file.

Suddenly the whole column was bunched together. The railroad track, or what remained of it, had been reached. The track, built by the French, had once connected Saigon and Hanoi, but much of it had been destroyed, and now only parts of it, such as the section that linked Da Nang to Phu Bai and Hue, were still in operation. Along this stretch the rails and crossties had disappeared. However, the grade was still evident as it wound through the hills.

The word was passed to spread out, as we had bunched up in what the Marines called a "cluster fuck." I backed off down the road, but not very far. I didn't want to lose sight of the others, and I didn't want to be left behind on the road when the column moved again. Some of the men sat down in the muddy road. I knelt to avoid getting my clothing dirty, but the longer we waited, the closer I seemed to draw to the others. Soon I could hear some of them whispering, "Where the hell is CUPP 4?"

A warning was passed. Everyone got quiet. Some of the men lay down. I could hear someone coming down the road from the opposite direction, the whisper of moving, and the soft plop of footsteps in the mud. Shivers walked down the road and called a challenge. It was CUPP 4.

There was whispered conversation as Lieutenant Smith tried to locate CUPP 5. Goyette did not know where they were. Smith called CUPP 5 on the radio and told them to move out, that they would have to catch up because he wasn't waiting with everyone standing around in a cluster. Smith tried to get the men moving again, but CUPP 4 and their PFs had gotten mixed with the C.P. group, and the men had to be separated and the file organized before we could move out.

At first the going was good along the track, and Lieutenant Smith set a fast pace. Then the column slowed, as a stream had to be crossed. The stream was not deep, and I jumped it to keep my boots dry. A few meters later we encountered the stream again. This time it was wider, and I tried to jump it in two steps so as to get only one boot wet. It was all in vain. A few minutes later the column plunged into the stream and waded along the channel. The stream was cold and swift, the bottom slick, and in spite of repeated warnings, men fell in the water with a splash.

A flare went off directly overhead, and with no place to go we froze, crouching in the water. There was nothing to do but stand naked and immobile, hoping there were no eyes to see. After the flare went out, it was several seconds before my night vision returned and I could see to move. I had taken only a few steps when another flare ignited.

Some patrol or observation post had detected our movement and reported it to the artillery battery at Baldy. It took several minutes for Smith to get the illumination stopped.

After a time Smith led us out of the stream. Water squished in my boots, and I was wet to the hips, but it made no difference because a heavy rain fell and the soft ground was quickly churned into mud by the passing feet.

Miserably we plodded on, the only comfort being that the rain drowned out some of the noise we made. Several times the column paused, for reasons that I never understood, and the Marines lay down and faced out, prepared for an attack. It was hard for me not to imagine every hill, every clump of trees that loomed out of the darkness, as a perfect site for an ambush. I could only imagine what thoughts were going through the point's mind.

Word was passed up the line that there was movement to the rear of the column. The column stopped, and the men fanned out in a halfhearted defensive effort. As everyone suspected, it was CUPP 5 catching up.

The stream was encountered again, but this time there was

a concrete bridge across it. The bridge had been blown, so that it collapsed in the middle and the center section was missing, making it necessary to walk precariously down the rain-slick concrete, jump over the missing section, and then climb up the equally slick far side.

After the bridge, the grade was in good condition, and quick movement was resumed. CUPP 4 dropped off, then CUPP 4 Minus — Sgt. "Rock" Waitulavich's team — dropped off. The C.P. group moved off the grade and into thick bushes, and CUPP 5 pushed on ahead. The rain was still falling, but it was a heavy mist now, and there was nothing to do but wait until it was light enough to see, light enough to risk a smoke.

Daylight came so imperceptibly through the thick gray clouds that I didn't even notice it. The trees slowly separated themselves from the darkness and became not a forest but a treeline along a rice paddy. Following the others, I pushed through wet, head-high bushes and stepped into the soft mud of the paddy. The field was enveloped in the mist, even the darkness of the treeline to our left vanishing into the gray. As we advanced through the gummy mud of the paddy, firing broke out on our right, followed by the thumping of grenades. Splashing through the mud, we tried to get out of the exposed field and into the shelter of the treeline. The treeline, or hedgerow, was an impenetrable wall of trees, thorns, vines, and brush growing out of a dike about four feet higher than the paddy. Unable to get into the trees, I hugged the side of the dike for protection.

"What the hell is going on?" Lieutenant Smith demanded. "Why don't they report what's going on?" Unaccountably Smith was receiving nothing over the radio. "Did you put in fresh batteries like I told you to?" The radio operator said he had and tried extra batteries that he was carrying.

Thinking that the treeline might be ruining his reception, Smith and his radioman splashed back through the paddy and climbed out on the railroad grade. Still he was unable to receive. Lieutenant McCay changed channels on his radio and sent it to Smith.

The firing had stopped as abruptly as it had begun. There was a single shot, silence, and then the firing broke out again with grenade explosions and, after about fifteen seconds, stopped. "It's

Rock," McCay's radioman called. "They ran into approximately thirty-five VC with packs and rifles. Two confirmed, two probables. The rest are running."

"Get in that treeline and block to the left," Smith called.

Sergeant Burris and Lieutenant McCay began hacking at the brush with Ka-Bar scout knives and crawled into the treeline. I followed them. Even then it was necessary to cut more vines and brush so that we could see out the other side.

Morning kept pushing back the darkness, but distant objects were still lost in the mist. A few feet from my side was an unoccupied VC bunker dug into the treeline. At the bottom of the bunker was a metallic object. I pointed it out to Burris and McCay. They said to leave it alone.

McCay called for artillery but was unable to get it because, although we could not see them, there were villes in the area. Lieutenant Smith called for close air support. Air support was considered more accurate and less likely to cause civilian casualties because of the judgment and control of the FAC (Forward Air Control) pilot, who could see dwellings which were invisible from the ground and might not appear or might be inaccurately marked on the maps.

Everything was quiet for a while, and then there were some muffled explosions. "They're blowing the bunkers in the ville," Smith called. "And they've found a rice cache. I'm going to send out small patrols to try and make contact and hold them until air gets here."

A runner came from CUPP 5 bringing a radio for Lieutenant Smith. He said that four or five suspected VC had walked through a group of PFs who made no attempt to stop them, crossed the railroad track, and disappeared. "It was probably their brothers," Lieutenant Smith said.

Instead of feeling at the center of everything, I had no idea what was going on. Burris and I decided to go with the CUPP 5 patrol. We followed the runner up the railroad track and joined the rest of the team. We stepped into the rice paddy behind a mine dog and began slogging our way forward.

The sun broke through the clouds, and for the first time we could see the kind of country we were in. It was a valley of wide rice fields, intersected by paddy dikes and bordered by hedgerows. The green valley was surrounded by low, rock-strewn, brush-lined hills, some of which appeared irregularly in the valley. We pushed through the paddy mud, which sucked at our boots, and climbed over the paddy dikes. In some palces we walked along the dikes, which made for easier walking but were more likely to be mined. The dog handler moved slowly along the dikes. He not only had to watch the dog, which would "alert" or signal when he spotted a mine or trip wire, but he also had to watch for ambush and snipers.

We came to a treeline, and the dog handler worked along the edges trying to find a way through it. He discovered a narrow, worn footpath. We followed the path through the treeline, and on the other side was a small ville composed of a dozen or so low-roofed, thatch hootches scattered in the trees. Women and children squatted in front of the hootches. There were no men.

The Marines spread out to search for rice or weapons caches, looking in the wells and poking cautiously in the piles of straw and rubbish. The ville, one of several scattered through the valley, was far from any sign of government authority. The Marines considered the villagers to be neutral. They didn't like either the government of South Vietnam or the Viet Cong. They just wanted to be left alone. The Viet Cong came to levy taxes on the rice and to conscript the young men. The Marines and PFs came to chase off the VC and to confiscate the rice the VC had collected so that they had to collect more.

The PFs had a simpler, less tolerant view of the ville. To the PF the enemy wasn't Hanoi or Communism, things about which he knew little. The enemy was the men of this ville who were hiding in the woods now instead of working their rice fields, and who would come out tonight to throw grenades at the PF's house and place booby traps along the paths where his children played.

"How many VC, mamasan?" the Marines asked.

"No bit," the women said.

Each house in the ville was equipped with a bunker, usually a mound of earth and rock with an entrance hole and a cavity inside, something like a dirt igloo. Because the VC sometimes took refuge in the bunkers, the Marines threw grenades in them. The grenades did not destroy the bunkers but killed or wounded anyone inside.

"Chieu hoi," the Marines called outside the bunkers. Literally meaning "open arms," the words were an appeal to return to the government. "Di-di mou," they called. (Get out.) After a few seconds, they called "fire in the hole," pulled the pin of a grenade while everyone else took cover, and threw the grenade into the bunker. The reason for taking cover was that sometimes a bunker contained explosives that, ignited by a grenade, not only destroyed the bunker but endangered anyone nearby.

Systematically the Marines worked their way through the ville, searching the hootches and blowing the bunkers. One of the bunkers blew apart, leaving little doubt what had been stored there.

After working their way through the ville, CUPP 5 was ordered to move into a blocking position, as Sergeant Rock had encountered the enemy again. Burris and I followed the team through the rice paddies and then along trails through the hedgerows. Firing broke out some distance ahead, so we moved faster, climbing on one of the hilltops for a better view. From the hill we had a clear view of escape routes through the lowland on either side. About five hundred meters to the front was a clump of trees or small woods that seemed to be covering a ravine. The Viet Cong had ducked into the trees.

The requested airplanes appeared overhead in the shape of four OV-10 Broncos. CUPP 5 was asked to put out air panels for identification, and Rock's team popped a green smoke grenade marking their position and threw a red smoke in the direction of the enemy. The OV-10s made a couple of passes over the suspected VC position without firing to be sure they were on the right target, and on the next pass came in with rockets. The airplanes made a coordinated attack, one pulling up just as the next began its run, giving the VC little opportunity to escape or to raise their heads to fire.

"Man, those are weird looking airplanes," said one grunt, referring to the twin-engine, prop-driven, slab-sided Broncos with their high boom tails and their oversize glass canopies. To men accustomed to sleek, streamlined jets, the OV-10 did look like something built by Mack Truck. But the Broncos, designed to do a variety of jobs—reconnaissance, search and rescue, medevac, weather check, forward air control, and close air support—were able to fly lower and slower than the jets and to hit pinpoint targets without endangering nearby troops.

The grunts sat down in a small field of sugarcane to watch

the show and open C rations. It was the first opportunity to eat since Burris and I had left the C.P., and I was hungry. The dog handler poured a canteen of water into his helmet for the dog to drink but fed him nothing because the dog had work to do. The PFs had no rations. Most of them went without eating, but two PFs slipped off to a small hootch, the thatched roof of which was barely visible under palm trees.

"Hey, where are you going?" one of the Marines called after them. "Come back here." They kept going.

In a few minutes I could hear a woman screaming from the direction of the hootch. "Boy, she's telling them," one of the Marines said. "Those old mamasans will fight the PFs." The two PFs reappeared carrying a pot between them. The old woman followed them a short way, screaming after them. Behind her was a column of smoke.

"They set her house on fire," a Marine said.

"That's number ten," the Marines said to the PFs in disapproval. The two PFs giggled in embarrassment and offered the Marines some of the food—fish no bigger than a man's finger boiled in rice. The Marines refused. The other PFs ignored both the food and the thieves.

"She jumped on them for stealing her food, so they set her house on fire," said one of the Marines. "They just turned her into a VC, but what can we do? The PFs get hungry too, but they don't get rations, and we don't have any authority to tell them what to do."

I turned to the other Marines, who shrugged. I tried to read their attitude to an intolerable situation over which they had no control. Were they indifferent? Frustrated? Angry? "It ain't real," one of them said. "It don't mean nothing." Denial had become the ultimate form of dealing with the unacceptable.

It was eleven o'clock, and the sun beat down unmercifully. "It'll be raining in five minutes," said one man, squinting at the sky. He was correct. A low cloud passed over the hill, and a heavy rain fell for about fifteen minutes. We put on helmets to keep the rain out of our faces and sat in the mud.

The OV-10s had finished their runs and had been circling, keeping the area under surveillance. They made one final low pass, waggled their wings, and left the area. CUPP 5 was told to hold its position while Rock's team swept through the wooded area.

"Yeah, we sit here in the mud while they get the glory," one of the Marines complained. With nothing else to do, some of the men chopped down stalks of sugarcane and chewed it. "It keeps you from getting thirsty, and it's the only thing over here that doesn't give you the shits."

"Look at that," a grunt said, pointing through the clouds at a jet flying high above us. "That's unreal. That's Pan Am with a bunch of tourists, and down here we're killing people." Few others bothered to look.

"There's a man down there," the dog handler said.

"Where?" asked an expert rifleman, chagrined that he hadn't seen him first.

"Right there. About a thousand meters. Wonder if I could drop him from here?"

The other members of the team began watching the man—I never did see him—and decided he was a farmer. "I could have dropped him with one shot from my M-16," said the dog handler. That brought an obscenity from the expert, who carried the older and heavier M-14. An argument began between the two men over which was the better rifle and degenerated into who was the better marksman. They cited scores fired at different ranges and issued invitations to step off five hundred meters and shoot it out.

"I can hit a target at a thousand meters with the M-14," said the expert. "You can't do that with an M-16."

"What can I say?" said the dog handler.

"I can drop an M-14 in a rice paddy, pick it up and fire it, and you can't do that with an M-16."

"What can I say?" said the dog handler.

The argument was interrupted by firing that broke out again, and CUPP 5 was ordered to move in the direction of fire. We walked off the hill and plunged into the rice paddies again. As there was another hill between us and the firing, there was some confusion as to which way we were to go. Finally, the dog handler, who was on the point, decided to walk over the top of the hill.

The rocky hill was barren except for small scrubby bushes I would expect in southern California or West Texas. The dog handler led the way through the brush, and when we were about halfway up the hill, the firing stopped. We kept going.

At the crest of the hill the dog alerted, and the handler called,

"Hold it." Everyone froze. "I've hit a wire," he said, and those closest to him cautiously backed away. Gingerly the handler reached down into the scrubby brush to feel for the booby trap. "It's just a loose wire," he said, and everyone relaxed. "Now don't go wandering around up here. This whole hilltop may be mined."

We walked single file until everyone was atop the hill. "Where the hell are we?" someone asked. There was no fighting, no VC, and no Marines. The countryside was quiet, peaceful, as though we had walked out of the war and into another time and place. The Marines checked the ground around them for mines and sat down. I did the same.

After a while Goyette climbed up the hill with CUPP 4. The men in CUPP 5 shouted warnings of mines, and CUPP 4 sat down with a minimum of moving about. The Marines from the two teams exchanged ideas of what was happening. "They are going to have to secure [conclude] this operation pretty soon if we are going to get back to the villes before dark," one of the grunts said.

"Yeah, just when everyone thinks it's all over, Rock will find them again." None of those on the hill had actually seen the VC all day.

Sure enough, Rock spotted the VC moving along a treeline, and CUPP 4 was ordered to sweep through the rice paddies, over an intervening hill, and to join the C.P. group on yet another hill. Burris and I decided to go with them.

The sun was blazing again, and the humidity was high. Because of the mortar attack and light probe, CUPP 4 had spent a sleepless night and had been on the move since 0430. Yet they splashed across the valley and panted up the hill. I tried in vain to keep up with them.

On the next hill we could see Lieutenant Smith waiting, and we plunged off the hill, walked across another valley—this one dry—and up the next hill. Some of the men, unable to keep up the pace, began to straggle. I slipped and stumbled up the steep hill, fell on the ground at the top, and pulled off the heavy flak jacket to let the air reach my sweat-drenched shirt.

Lieutenant Smith pointed out to Goyette the treeline into which the VC had disappeared. Smith had called for air support again, and CUPP 4 got a respite. We sprawled on the ground gasping for breath. A heavy downpour fell again, and it was necessary to stand to avoid the rivulets of water running off the hill.

An old man appeared carrying a dead dog. Bowing and weeping, he lay the dog before Lieutenant Smith, hoping to be compensated for it. Smith eyed the dog suspiciously. "Is this your dog? Belong to you?" The old man nodded, bowing and weeping. "Where's the bullet hole?" Smith asked, poking at the dog with his foot. "How do I know who killed the dog? There's not even a bullet hole? Did you kill the dog?"

Uncomprehending, the old man continued bowing and weeping.

"Hell, he's going to eat it anyway," Shivers said. "He probably killed it himself."

Smith called the corpsman over to examine the dog. "He's dead," the corpsman said.

"I know he's dead; what did he die of?"

The corpsman examined the dog and shrugged.

"I don't know who killed your dog," Smith said to the old man, refusing to pay. The man left, dragging the dog by an ear.

The rain slackened and helicopters arrived, two sharklike Cobra gunships and an old reliable Huey. The two Cobras made rocket runs on the treeline while the Huey circled inside their pattern as air control. The Cobras were faster and more heavily armed than the utilitarian Hueys. There was a joke about the survivor of an NVA unit looking at his dazed and dying buddies and saying, "Don't shoot at the shark-nosed bird."

"I see somebody," Goyette said. "There's a man coming out of the treeline."

"I can drop him from here," said one Marine aiming his M-16. Several other Marines also took aim, but the helicopter had spotted the man, and the Huey swung around, giving the door gunner a shot. The man went down in a spray of bullets from the door gunner's M-60 machine gun. The Marines on the hill cheered.

"God damn, you don't often get to see somebody dropped out in the open like that," Shivers said.

"Man, he had balls walking out in the open like that," Goyette said. Others thought the man had been addled or terrified by the rockets and had stumbled out in the open.

"What do you want to bet the body is gone by the time we

get there," said one Marine, a veteran of the bush war. "Even with people up here watching it."

Lieutenant Smith wanted CUPP 4 to circle around the left flank of the treeline, check out a ville hidden in a tropical forest behind the hills, and then sweep through the treeline where the VC had been.

We pushed off the hill as the rain fell. We had reached the end of the valley, and here there were no rice fields but hills and marshes covered with trees and vines and rank stands of bamboo. A single footpath ran through the junglelike vegetation. The patrol came to a stop. Somehow the radioman had failed to get the word and was still atop the hill with the C.P. group. A runner was sent to get him.

No one liked the area we were in. It was impossible to see into the tangles of brush, and no one liked standing around. Goyette passed the word for the men to spread out along the trail and to keep moving. The radioman would have to catch up.

Ahead, hidden beneath the trees, were scattered houses, some of them with masonry walls and tile roofs. One of the things I had never been able to understand in the news I read and saw back home was how Americans could bomb or shoot into villages, or how the Viet Cong could rocket a base or a city, without being seen. I was getting some answers. I had been told there was a ville and that we were going to sweep through it, yet I was almost in it before I saw it. We were in heavy, almost impenetrable brush in an area that had remained almost unchanged for a hundred years. In America citizens might argue the relative merits of Nguyen Van Thieu and Nyugen Cao Ky; here the villagers were unlikely to have heard of either.

The Marines encircled the first masonry house, and one man cautiously looked in the door. The house was deserted. The Marines poked about the yard looking for weapons and rice caches. An American steel helmet lay rusting on the ground. No one touched it. While the Marines searched around the house, the radioman caught up. Staff Sergeant Shivers was with him.

Around the houses the ground was more open, with paths through the brush and even small garden plots. I felt naked walking through the ville without a weapon, especially when often there was not another human in sight. With my camera inside my flak jacket to keep the film dry, I had nothing to occupy my hands. Besides, I had grown up in the wide open spaces of north-west Texas, and I felt a touch of claustrophobia in the close, narrow spaces of the trail. In the rice paddies we had been a unit, and I had felt a sense of security in being part of a large target. In the ville, the Marines and PFs had spread out around the trails and hootches, so that every man was an individual target. And the range was extremely close. If I became a target, I didn't see how the VC could miss or how Burris or any other Marine could have time to help me.

I thought of how inviting a target I might seem to some VC hiding in the bush or one of the hootches as we closed in around him. Generally in the military, the lower the rank, the bigger the weapon. It occurred to me that without a rifle I might look like an officer, and I had heard that the Viet Cong, particularly Viet Cong snipers, preferred officers for targets. I wished I were back on the hill with the C.P. group—but I was in the ville, and there was no way out except with the others. I chose to stick close to Shivers, trusting that Burris would cover my back as we worked our way to the next house.

This house was also masonry with wooden doors—an uncommon sight in the area. "Chieu hoi," Shivers called out. "Di-di mou." He knelt beside the wall, fired a burst from the grease gun that splintered the door, kicked it open, and stepped inside. This house was also empty, and the floor was littered with rubble —rocks and mortar that had fallen from the walls, and broken tile from the shattered roof. Shivers poked through the rubble for trapdoors and walked out the far side of the house. I followed close behind him.

Outside was a large bunker covered with stones. After calling a warning first in Vietnamese and then in English, Shivers threw a grenade into the bunker. "Get down," he yelled, running a few paces and then dropping himself. The bunker entrance had a right-angle turn to prevent anyone from firing directly into it. Shivers's grenade had hit the wall and rolled back outside. Shrapnel rattled against the masonry wall of the hootch I had crouched behind, but no one was injured. Shivers placed the next grenade well back into the inside of the bunker.

The rain had become increasingly heavy until it was a tropical downpour, falling in sheets so thick that visibility was cut to a few meters. Through the rain loomed another house, this one a typical thatch hootch built on bamboo poles but having a concrete floor. One wall had been removed, and in the opening sat an old, wrinkled, gray-haired woman and a three- or four-year-old girl. These were the only two people discovered in the ville.

"Lau dai," Shivers called to the woman. (Come here.) Instead of obeying, she began to wail. "Di-di mou," he called. Still she didn't move. Goyette went into the house, took the woman by the arm, and led her outside with the child. She stood cringing and wailing in the rain. There was a trapdoor in the concrete floor that led to an underground bunker. "Get the old woman and the kid away," Shivers said. "I'm going to blow this bunker."

Goyette pushed the old woman and the child down the trail. The woman wailed; the child looked bewildered. Despite Goyette's attempt at gentleness, both the woman and child were terrified. No one knew whether it was because she thought she would be killed or her house burned, or perhaps because there was someone in the bunker.

When the woman and the child were safely away, Shivers called out warnings to surrender or come out and dropped a grenade through the trapdoor. The woman was released, but instead of returning to the hootch with the child, she stood crying in the rain. Goyette and Shivers moved on. I followed them.

Once past the houses we entered a marshy, jungled area with vegetation so thick the only passage was on footpaths. Half-sunk in the spongy earth was a rusting tank, of Japanese or French vintage, with moss growing on its sides and vines and creepers emerging through its ports. One Marine found a fresh footprint, nothing more. Just off one of the paths was a bunker with three small sticks stuck upright in the opening—the sign of a booby trap. Slowly we pushed along the slippery footpaths. Streams of water poured off the broad-leaf trees.

Abruptly we were out of the marsh and at the edge of a rice field. There was cover and good footing close to the trees, but soon we were back plodding through the paddy toward another treeline. There was a trail along the treeline and an opening through the trees to another paddy, and on the other side of that field, another treeline. That treeline was where the VC had taken refuge from the Cobras. One man had run into the open and had been shot, but there was no body. There was a cone hat and a hoe in the rice field. Any blood had probably been washed away in the downpour. There were small, irregular white grains. Someone identified them for me as bits of shattered bone. Under the trees was a trench which ran the entire length of the treeline.

When the sweep through the treeline was completed, Lieutenant Smith called an end to the operation. CUPP 5 and the C.P. group had already started back to their area. CUPP 4 waded across the rice paddies to join them.

Lieutenant Smith radioed for hot chow to be waiting at the C.P. for his platoon. "It's going to be dark by the time they get back to the ville and get cleaned up. At least they won't have to take time to heat their rations," he said.

We walked along the side of a hill until we came to a stream —the same stream we had crossed several times in the darkness of the morning—and we waded across it again. The rain slackened and then stopped, but no one cared any more. We were soaked to the skin. My feet, which had been wet from the first time we had crossed the stream, were puffed and tender, the skin wrinkled like a raisin.

"Before we got here, the Army ran an armored ambush in the same area we were in today. An armored ambush," Smith said in disgust. "They didn't get shit. The gooks heard them coming two days away." -

We broke through one treeline to find a man plowing his field with a water buffalo, seemingly oblivious to all the shooting that had been going on. He appeared to be about thirty, military age, the first such Vietnamese male anyone had seen all day who was not a PF. "Lau dai," Shivers called him over. The man seemed willing enough, but the buffalo began thrashing and plunging about. The buffalo did not like Americans.

"Lau dai," Shivers called again, and a couple of Marines raised their rifles to cover the buffalo. Everyone had heard stories of Americans being killed by the bulls. A young girl appeared from nowhere, took the bull, and led it away with ease. "That's not even his bull," Shivers said. "That bull doesn't even know him."

The plowman came over. Shivers eyed him suspiciously. He pulled up the man's shirt. The plowman had a fresh but minor wound. Lieutenant Smith called the PF honcho over to talk to the plowman. The man explained to the honcho that he had scratched himself walking through the treeline. The honcho said the man was OK.

Lieutenant Smith detailed two Marines to drop off into the trees and watch the man. If the plowman di-died, they were to waste him. The man went back to plowing and lived. Shivers remained unconvinced.

We slogged on through the mud and stopped at the foot of the hill below the platoon C.P. The hot food had not arrived. The Marines collapsed on the muddy ground, and while Lieutenant Smith and the team leaders went over the operation for the report to Captain Tilley, the grunts made their own assessment of the day's work.

"We chased them all day, and how many do you think we got?"

"Hell, I saw two bodies, and I saw two more go down, but I didn't have time to look for them."

"You wouldn't have found them anyway. Unless you shoot them out in the open, you'll never find the bodies, no matter how dead they are."

"How about that guy the helicopter gunner shot? He was in the open and we couldn't find him."

"Is that what you wanted?" a Marine asked me. "Can you get a story out of that?"

"Body count" was a sore subject in Vietnam. Finding and bringing in VC bodies was onerous and often dangerous work because the bodies were sometimes booby-trapped. At other times ambushes were set up around the bodies. Some grunts blamed the chore of bringing in enemy bodies on the press corps, and it was true that some photographers wanted to photograph the bodies, and some reporters asked for a body count and would not report it unless they could personally verify it. But it was the military report that required a body count.

I had been asked that day if I wanted to see the bodies and had declined, but Lieutenant Smith needed the body count for his report. After conferring with McDonnell, McCay, and Sergeant Shivers, he decided to claim four kills—the two bodies that had been recovered and the others that several men had seen during the firefight but could not find afterward. The man shot by the door gunner was left to the helicopter to claim, along with two others they had spotted from the air. Seven confirmed kills.

Lieutenant Smith called for the two packs taken from the recovered bodies and examined them. They contained a packet of coarse brown rice and a plastic bag of long-grain rice. "That's American rice," he said. There was also some coarse tobacco twisted up in a banana leaf, a packet of pills that the corpsman identified as VC malaria pills, a hammock which the VC used to stay off the wet ground, and a U.S. Army manual. "That must be a big help to them," Smith said in disgust.

The jeep arrived with a trailer of hot chow as rain fell again. No one bothered to curse. They lined up around the trailer to fill paper plates with hamburger patties, thick slabs of bread, stewed tomatoes, lima beans, ice cream, and iced tea. The CUPP leaders waited until their men had been fed, and Lieutenant Smith waited to be the last man served. Marine tradition is that no officer in the field eats until his men have been fed. After Lieutenant Smith filled his plate, he asked if anyone wanted any more and then distributed the remainder of the food to the PFs who had also been in the field all day.

Like men anywhere, as they ate they talked about work and the job they had done that day. Only the new men in the teams were happy; they had survived and that was enough. Among the "short timers," those who had been there long enough to count the days remaining, the attitude ranged from disappointment to frustration.

"Like most battles of the Vietnam War, it was prolonged, exhausting, and indecisive," a Marine pretended to quote from the story he imagined I was going to write.

As a member of the media, I was regarded as more than a presence; I was seen as a determinant. Nothing that happened in Vietnam was real, only what happened back home. Therefore, failure or success did not depend on the living and dying the soldiers did, the killing and saving, but on how it was reported back home.

The real "hearts and minds" campaign was not directed at Vietnamese peasants but at the American media. And it was not waged only at MAC-V and JUSPAO. Every grunt, knowingly or intuitively, tried to affect the media's slant for or against the war. Almost everyone from general to grunt had a ready supply of aphorisms honed and polished. Everyone wanted to capture the attention of the media for a moment. Few seemed to believe they could do so by heroic action; many seemed to believe they

could grab the spotlight by saying what the media wanted to hear.
The unreality of the war was such that everyone wanted some
proof they had been there. Cameras were everywhere. Pilots took
pictures of their bombs on the target for folks back home; grunts
took snapshots of their buddies killing and being killed. But the
most highly sought prize of all, replacing the Congressional
Medal of Honor, was for ten seconds to be an anonymous face
in America's living rooms saying, "Like most battles of the Vietnam War, it was prolonged, exhausting, and indecisive."

"I want you to take these men back to their villes," Lieutenant Smith told the driver. "They're humped enough for today."

CUPP 4 picked up their weapons and climbed into the trailer
for a ride back to the ville. Few of them planned to change into
dry clothes. Once they were back in the ville, they would move
into their night position, and the rain had left water standing
in the fighting holes where they would spend the night.

I did not go with them, although I could have. Spending a
night in the rain, moving every two or three hours from one mud-
filled hole to the next, was part of their experience I did not
want to share.

"All we did today was make Charlie mad," Corporal Goyette
told his men as they got in the truck. "He'll hit us tonight."

"The old man is going to be mad as hell," Smith confided to
Shivers and Waitulavich. "Keeping these men out all day and getting only seven confirmed."

Both were wrong. CUPP 4 wasn't hit that night, and Captain
Tilley wasn't angry over the results of the operation. They had
chased the VC out of the valley, at least temporarily, they had
captured a rice cache, and they had suffered no casualties. Captain Tilley was proud of his men. "They're outnumbered, they're
in the open, and they're vulnerable," he said. "God, they're vulnerable. Those small teams can be overrun at any time. So far
the VC have found it too costly.

"Out there the Marines develop animal senses. They stay alert.
They move. They react. They counterattack. They don't develop
a defensive attitude. They don't trust in barbed wire and bunkers. And so far they've been successful."

There was a barbed-wire-and-bunker mental complex in Vietnam. I had seen it in Phu Bai and Quang Tri, where men huddled in sandbagged hootches listening to rock music on Japa-

nese stereos, trying to shut out everything beyond the wire. In their mind there was the music and "the world." "The world" was everything they dreamed of, everything they remembered of what they had left. They had an expression for anything outside the wire and outside "the world." "It ain't real," they said.

Air

Sergeant Burris and I hitched a ride on the back of a ROK Marine truck carrying a load of grenades and spent the night in the relative comfort and safety of Da Nang. Safe, that is, relative to New York, Los Angeles, or Houston. I returned to the press center, where I rewarded myself with a hot shower, fresh clothes, a steak, and a drink that the press center called "a dirty mother," composed of milk, crème de cacao, and scotch.

Afterward, I sat on the basketball court and watched a movie, shown on the wall of the mess hootch. A Vietnamese patrol boat went up the river tossing grenades to prevent VC frogmen from blowing up the bridge, and occasionally a sentry on the bridge fired a stream of tracers at something suspicious in the water. All in all, the superficial Hollywood concoction showing on the wall seemed more real than the sampans floating on the river.

The next morning I asked to interview the Bronco pilots who had supported Third Platoon the day before. I wanted to get an idea of how it looked from the air. I was taken to VMO 2, the Marine Observation Squadron on the sprawling Da Nang air base.

I was unable to talk to the men who had flown air cover for Third Platoon, but was given Lt. Tom Hudson, of Carmel, California. I waited in a hangar, watching off-duty Marines playing volleyball. Lieutenant Hudson was busy. He spent four to six hours a day, seven days a week, on administrative duties as Assistant Administrative Officer, R and R Officer, Postal Officer, Information Service Officer, Directives Control, and Administrative Reports Control. It was hard to imagine the Red Baron, or Joe Foss, pushing papers for four to six hours a day.

My first impression of Lieutenant Hudson was of a man in a hurry; a tall, bright, successful businessman, perhaps a young lawyer on his way to becoming district attorney. Hudson averaged a little over two hours a day in the air. In good flying weather he flew two or three hops a day and caught up on his paperwork at night.

Whatever free time Hudson had, seemed to be spent talking flying and making and improving can guns. As we walked to his hootch, we had to dodge projectiles from several of the guns. The guns were made by cutting the ends out of C-ration cans and taping them end to end, one end remaining closed. A tennis ball was then shoved into the open end of the taped cans, and lighter fluid was squirted into a small hole in the closed end. After a classified number of seconds to allow the fluid to mix with oxygen and become volatile, the fuel was ignited, and the resulting explosion propelled the tennis ball a surprising distance with respectable force. Shoots-outs between hootches were common, as were ambushes of unwary pilots returning from missions or the Officers' Club.

"You've got to watch it through here," Hudson said. "This is Indian Country. They have a six-can gun in that hootch over there." We walked into his hootch as tennis balls bounced off the wall around us.

"Did they get you?" asked a short, round-faced captain with quick eyes and tight smile.

"They missed," Hudson sneered. "With all six shots."

The captain was taping together a very long can gun. "They go in for firepower over there," the captain said. "We go in for accuracy." He poked the can gun out the door, took aim at the sign on the opposite hootch, and fired. The ball hit the sign, which rocked slowly forward and fell to the ground.

"Stand by for BDA [Bomb Damage Assessment]," Hudson said solemnly. "One hundred percent on target. One hundred percent destruction."

"Thank you much," the captain replied.

When I made a remark about the ungainly bird he flew, Lieutenant Hudson was quick to come to its defense. The OV-10 was a STOL (short takeoff and landing) airplane, designed for use on dirt roads and rough, unimproved fields. In Vietnam, the Marines didn't have to worry about that, as they operated from fields built to accommodate jets. Instead, they landed long and hot and strapped all the ordnance they could get on the stubby-winged plane.

"Actually the OV-10 is underpowered for the load of ordnance we carry," Hudson said. "You have to think ahead to stay out of a low-power situation, and losing an engine with all that weight is critical."

Hudson was jet-qualified and carrier-qualified, but unlike some of his friends, he was not disappointed when he received orders to fly the Bronco. "I could foresee what would happen," he said. "We'd be around longer. Average sixty-five or seventy hours of flying a month. We talk about who gets to fly tomorrow; the jet pilots talk about who gets to fly this month. They get no picture of what's happening on the ground. They see a mark and hit it. Flying the OV-10 is the most interesting and challenging job in Vietnam." Hudson thought about that for a moment. "Well, I'd rather be fighting MiGs over North Vietnam, but flying the Bronco is interesting and challenging. It's been an enjoyable tour. A new experience."

To explain what made flying the Bronco so challenging, Hudson introduced me to his AO (aerial observer), Lt. Mike Cerre, of Grosse Pointe, Michigan. Cerre, a former tank commander, was shorter, darker, and more muscular than Hudson. All aerial observers were infantry or tank officers who understood the situation on the ground, the likely disposition of the troops, and what the troops might be expected to do.

"The grunts are almost always under cover, lying in treelines or along paddy dikes," Cerre said. "They're hard to see from the air, they're scattered, and they may be on several sides of a target area."

We're an airborne communications system," Cerre said. Cerre talked to the ground troops and artillery while Hudson talked to helicopters and fixed-wing aircraft. They also talked to each other while Cerre watched the ground and Hudson watched the ground, flew the airplane, and made rocket and machine-gun runs. "It's a matter of coordination," Cerre said. "There may be helicopters, fixed-wing aircraft, artillery, and ground all talking at the same time, plus extraneous radio traffic. You have to get straight in your mind what you're going to do, and shut out what you don't want to hear."

Hudson said when the radio traffic got too heavy he sometimes keyed the mike while firing his machine guns so they could hear the sound of the guns. "They get the message," he said.

The division sent down fragmentary orders, or "frag sheets," the night before a mission, and Hudson and Cerre were alerted and given the approximate ordnance they would be carrying. They received their mission number in the air. "We react to situations," Hudson said. "That's the challenge. We plan the mission in the air, maybe in bad weather, with people shooting at us, while trying to avoid friendly artillery fire or giving away the position of the troops on the ground."

"We support Marines," Cerre said.

"And other friendlies," Hudson added.

To improve their communication, Hudson and Cerre tape-recorded every mission and played it back afterward and discussed what they had done, how clear a picture they had of what was happening, and what they could have done better. "We have to be sure we're talking about the same target," Cerre said.

"There's a new twist to every mission," Cerre said. "You never learn it all. We get a lot of feedback from the other pilots and AOs, and we try to learn from their experience."

Hudson told of a mission in support of a Marine reconnaissance team. The teams were small, six to nine men, and operating in enemy territory. The pilots knew the approximate grid of every recon team and responded to their calls. One team laid an air panel in a stream bed and asked Hudson to fire to the north of it.

"Where are bad guys?" Hudson asked.

"North side of blue line," recon answered. "Blue line" was a stream or river, which was marked blue on military maps.

"They were excited, I was excited, and I forgot to ask their position. 'Get in a hole, I'm going to fire,' I told them, rolling in and hitting the target with machine guns. 'How was that?' 'Outstanding,' recon said, 'You want to hear them screaming?' I said, 'State your pos.' 'Five meters south of blue line.' Holy shit, I had fired right over their heads."

"It's great to know you helped a recon team," Cerre said. "You can hear them whispering in the mike and you know there's bad guys all around. Usually when they get into contact it's at very close range."

"We like to work with them because they're close together, they are the only friendlies in an area that has already been cleared for fire, and they are very professional on the radio," Hudson said.

They agreed the most difficult mission was supporting ground troops that were scattered over a wide area and coordinating air support, artillery support, and medevacs. We went to Hudson's office and listened to a tape they had recorded of a recent mission. The first time through, I heard only a confusion of voices and unfamiliar words. It was some time before I was able to recognize Hudson and Cerre's voices and to filter out extraneous traffic.

"Where are bad guys from your pos?" Cerre asked the commander of the ground troops, whose view was limited to the immediate horizon.

"We have sightings on that ridgeline."

"Are you talking of ridgeline to our ten o'clock?" Cerre asked.

"That ridgeline to my right."

Right and *left* meant nothing to Hudson and Cerre, who had no idea which way the grunts were facing. Hudson circled while Cerre studied his chart. "That's Hill 214?" Cerre asked.

"Roger that. We spotted people moving down west side of slope."

"Are friendlies out of the area?"

"Most affirm. Hill 214, no friendlies."

"Roger, I copy," Cerre responded.

Next was the voice of Hudson calling an air strike. "Ringneck, this is Hostage Eagle. We need your pad. Scramble F4s. Snake and retard bombs or napalm."

In the meantime Cerre was alerting artillery to the air strike. High-arcing artillery shells could knock down an airplane. Artillery responded, "Recline Echo. We have a 'Save a Plane' in your area. LZ Dagger, impacting 7947, max ord ten point eight. LZ Dagger, impacting 1943, max ord five point seven. Hill 65, impacting 8144, max ord four point zero."

Lieutenant Cerre stopped the tape player and explained. "They were giving me the location of the guns, the impact area, and the maximum elevation of the ordnance fired."

"Recline Echo, check fire last two named for one zero minutes." Cerre asked artillery to discontinue fire for ten minutes.

"Was movement to southern edge?" Cerre asked ground troops.

"Roger that. Top of hill, down hill, across blue line to southwest. Lost sight of them when they moved into treeline. Will try to get arty on hill. Understand danger factor here with planes."

"Roger, if you'll stand by. Any contact at this time?"

"Negative. Request two emergency medevacs. Zone not secure."

"Working on medevac for you," Hudson said. "Scrambled air, three point zero, three point five minutes. Medevac two zero minutes. Slick someone to check LZ."

Other voices floated in and out of the conversation. "Joker One, this is Joker Leader, are you in contact?"

"Check fire, check fire, friendlies in area."

"Roger, I got your flash. Coming in to west with twenty mike mike."

"Popping willie peter. Gooners fifteen meters south of willie peter."

"You have to ignore all that," Hudson said.

"It sounds interesting."

"It always sounds interesting. But you have to get a clear picture of what you're going to do, and you have to hold that picture in your mind."

"How far west patrol going to move?" Cerre asked ground. The main unit had sent out a patrol, and Cerre was trying to locate them before air arrived.

"Held up three hundred meters to the west. Going to take a look at what it's like in the area. Fire mission this morning had secondaries and two sightings. You might want to take a look."

"Roger, we'll check it out."

An earlier artillery mission had hit ammo caches, causing secondary explosions and troop movement. Hudson and Cerre made a visual reconnaissance of the area checking for hootches, trenches, bunkers, or bodies that the artillery fire might have uncovered. Meanwhile Cerre contacted artillery and requested a firing mission. Artillery read back the grid coordinates. "You have correct copy. Get that cleared for one thousand meters. We want to walk it around in there. Like to use mixed delay."

The jet aircraft reported on station.

"The first consideration in laying down ordnance is friendly troops; the second is terrain," Hudson said. Terrain was the danger factor the ground commander had referred to earlier. The jets, moving at better than ten miles a minute, had a poor picture of what was taking place on the ground. In a dive, while concentrating on the target, the pilots did not see much dimension, and Hudson had to direct the jets so they could effectively hit the target without endangering friendly troops, and without flying into a mountain.

The most important information was run-in heading and direction of pulloff. "Attack bearing zero two zero with right-hand pulloff. Friendlies at eight o'clock." Hudson made certain that no friendlies were at six or twelve o'clock, where a bomb that went short, long, or skipped could hit them. He gave the local weather—"four thousand broken"—described the target, what he had seen, and the target elevation. A few feet of elevation made a difference to the fast movers with high-dive ordnance. "Mountains rising ten to twelve o'clock."

Hudson told the jets where he would be while they were making their runs, how he was going to mark the target, how he wanted them to place the ordnance on the target, and in how many runs. "Napalm first, snake eyes in two passes." Hudson did not want the jets to make more than three runs on a hot target.

The jet pilots read back the information to reduce the margin of error. "You have correct copy. Rolling in to mark target," Hudson said, marking the target with smoke. "Do you have sighting?"

"Roger, have tally," the jets replied. If they did not see the marking, they responded, "No joy."

Cerre asked the ground commander how the marking looked. "Looks good," ground responded. "Right on target." The smoke became the target reference.

"Where do you want ordnance?" the jets asked.

"Place right on smoke. Work western slope to north."

Hudson turned off the tape for more explaining. "I fly a pattern over the friendly troops to keep the gun plane from accidentally turning in on them," he said.

"It also keeps us out of enemy gunfire," Cerre added.

"I fly inside the jets' pattern, turning with them to keep them in visual contact, and staying either lower or higher than they are so I can be certain that they are on a run-in heading and that their wings are level. I ask myself, 'Does the aircraft setup look right for the target? Does the pilot sound as though he's sure of the target.' They don't have much of a picture."

He turned the tape player on. "Turning base, tally on target," the jet called.

"Roger, continue."

"Turning in hot."

"Roger, continue, looking good."

Hudson stopped the player. "This is the critical moment. He has turned on his final bomb run. I have to determine whether or not he is on a proper approach and if he is cleared to drop his bombs. I give him 'cleared hot' or I call, 'abort, abort, abort,' and bring him in on another approach."

Hudson called, "Cleared hot. Got two away."

"That's to let him know his systems are working. Then I turn back into the pattern to pick up the next jet coming in for a run. After they make their runs, I advise them to stay high, and we go down for a look."

Flying somewhere between three hundred feet and the tree-tops, and slowing the airplane, Hudson and Cerre look for anything uncovered by the bombing. "We present a good target, so I fire my machine guns to keep their heads down," Hudson said. "If we're shot at it's usually just after we've passed over the target area. We don't often hear gunfire or see muzzle flashes. Ground has to tell us if we're being fired on."

Cerre said, "I'm in contact with ground, so I get their opinion on how well the bombs were on target."

"We didn't see any new targets, so I had the jets continue to work over the entire area. Sometimes I have to re-mark the area, but in this case there was a cloud of dust over the target, so I used it as the target reference."

Hudson snapped on the recorder. "Cover entire target area with pistol."

"They've dropped their ordnance, and I'm calling for their twenty-millimeter cannon. When they expend that they report, 'Going high and dry,' or sometimes they say, 'Winchester.'"

There were more voices fading in and out, and then I could detect Hudson saying, "Roger, stand by for BDA."

"I take another look at the target area and give them a bomb damage assessment—time on and off the target, ordnance used, grid for the target they hit, unit they supported, and a grade for the percentage of bombs on the target and the percentage of destruction. In this case I gave them 100 percent on target, 100 percent destruction."

"Thank you much," the jets responded. "Very fine air strike control."

"Are you checking LZ?" Cerre asked ground.

"Roger, have sighting on it."

"How many pas [passengers]?"

"Two WA coming out."

"Two, roger. How does LZ look?"

"Wait one," ground responded asking for a minute to check out the zone. "LZ good. Approach southeast."

"Roger, copy that."

The medevac package of two Cobra helicopter gunships and two CH-46 Sky Knight medevac helicopters reported on station. One Sky Knight was the rescue bird and stayed high for an emergency pickup in the event the other was hit. Hudson gave them an LZ brief—best approach, direction and velocity of wind, number of passengers, nature of wounds, position of last enemy contact, and how long ago.

Hudson made a visual rendezvous with the lead Cobra, Scarface Two One. "Have you over blue line in left bank."

"That's affirm."

Hudson then went high to act as extra cover if needed, or to lay smoke screen if the zone got hot.

Cerre contacted ground. "Work with Scarface Two One. Start WA out of area now. If receive fire, pop your smoke. Anytime you hear fire from ground let us know."

"Roger that. Wounded Oscar Mike [on the move]."

Hudson and Cerre circled, watching for enemy movement. The pickup medevac touched down only briefly. "Wounded out at this time," they reported.

"All wounded aboard?"

"Affirm, all aboard."

"Two WA aboard?"

"That's affirm."

Cerre punched off the recorder. "That's crucial. You don't want to leave somebody and have to go back. Choppers draw too much fire."

"Recline, ready for mission?" Cerre called artillery.

"Roger, have clearance," artillery replied, giving information on the ordnance fired, time of flight, and maximum trajectory. Lieutenant Hudson flew a horseshoe pattern that kept the Bronco out of the way but kept Lieutenant Cerre in a position to observe until the firing mission was complete.

The Broncho returned to base. It was not yet time for lunch, but the day's flying was over and the paperwork waited.

On the ground I had felt confused and nearsighted. Like a person of short stature, I had believed that if I could see beyond that treeline, over that hill, then I would know. I would have some understanding of what I was up against, what would be demanded of me. After listening to the tapes, I wasn't sure that air had a picture either. Dropping bombs at smoke drifting through the trees, flying over friendlies to prevent jets from turning in on them, or looking for air panels to discover the disposition of troops was not reassuring.

I was awed by the speed and power that air support represented but doubt persisted. I confessed to Hudson and Cerre that I didn't like the idea of lying on the ground while supersonic jets dropped bombs at smoke that dissipated in the wind and trees.

"We allow a meter a pound as a safety factor," Cerre said. "Five-hundred-pound bomb, five hundred meters from troops."

"The big nightmare is hitting friendly troops," Lieutenant Hudson confessed. "I was FAC for a jet that dropped a bomb long. No one was hit, but it was my responsibility. They're my bombs until they hit the deck."

Lieutenant Cerre came to the defense of air support. "It's not always the pilot's fault when something goes wrong," he said. "On the ground they're getting shot at, and their wounded are screaming, and they're excited—and that can get someone hurt. Sometimes ground gives you bad information."

"You have to get straight in your mind what you're going to do," Hudson said.

"And what if you have what you're going to do straight in your mind but your picture is based on bad information?" I asked.

"Somebody's going to get hurt," Hudson said.

Second Platoon

The return trip to Golf CUPP was made with Corporal Hinkle. Sergeant Burris, who was a one-digit midget with less than ten days remaining in Vietnam, had asked to go back with me, but Lieutenant Waldrop had rightly refused permission. "He's too short to be going out there," Waldrop said, detailing Hinkle instead.

Staff Sergeant Merriman took Hinkle and me up to the general's pad overlooking the headquarters of the First Marine Division and the city and bay of Da Nang. Da Nang, a city of half a million people, had quadrupled in size since 1960, but it was still rural in character with no newspaper, no taxi service, no sewage system, and only one public telephone. Small, ramshackle houses were built everywhere—on islands in the river, on poles in the shallow end of the bay. Farther out in the deep water of the bay were a couple of destroyers and the ghost-white hospital ship *Sanctuary*.

Waiting on the pad was a CH-46 chopper called a Chinook by the Army and a Sea Knight by the Marines. This one was a Sea Knight with two young Marine pilots, Lieutenants Forbush and Tucker, of the let's-get-this-thing-in-the-air-and-see-what-happens type usually encountered only in World War I movies. They greeted us with smiles and handshakes as though they were going to try to sell us the helicopter, ushered us aboard, and presented us with business cards: "This trip courtesy of the Purple Foxes," complete with a Disneyesque purple fox and the motto "Give a shit."

With a high-pitched whine the rotors wound up and we lifted off. Leaving the city behind, the chopper dropped low over the Cu De River. The jagged marble mountain and the beaches along the South China Sea appeared in the opposite port. I turned for a look out of the port behind me and saw signs of an incredible battle. Below was a tiny ville, and surrounding the ville were hundreds of bomb and shell craters—Vietnam as described in the newspapers. I had not seen any bomb craters from the ground, and this was my first glimpse of them from the air.

I took several photographs of the ville, mentally writing phrases such as "the pitted earth" and "scarred like the face of the moon."

"Graves," said Corporal Hinkle.

"Huh?"

"The Buddhists bury you standing up, and the grave is a circle like a womb. Mother Earth or something like that. If you look real close you can see where they have little openings in the circle. When you're reborn you come out of the womb, and you've got to have an opening."

Sure enough, there were womblike circles with openings.

"If you look there are probably people down there working on them. They fix them up for Tet. Pull up the weeds and put fresh dirt on them."

I could see people working on the craters. I put away the camera.

"No telling how many generations are buried there. Everywhere you look there are graves. A lot of correspondents think those are bomb craters. They take pictures of them and report that the craters go right into the village."

I pretended to laugh with Hinkle.

When we arrived at the Golf Company C.P., Captain Tilley was on R and R in Hawaii. Lieutenant Hess, the company executive officer, was acting C.O. Golf 2 (Second Platoon) had an operation planned the next day with CUPP 8 and 10 and we were invited along. Hinkle and I went outside to wait for the Second Platoon jeep.

Staff Sergeant Shivers came limping over. "You should have stuck around. Things got real exciting after you left," he said, pointing at the leg that had earned him his fifth "purple hurt"— the one that was going to send him home.

Lieutenant McDonnell also came over, limping slightly and self-consciously tonguing the stitches in his upper lip and the gap where his front teeth had been knocked out by grenade fragments. "You really missed it," he said.

Both men had been wounded a few days after I left when the VC broke through the wire and assaulted the Third Platoon C.P. bunker with grenades. The PFs and PSDFs stayed in their places and fought. "We could hear them screaming and crying but they didn't di-di," Shivers said.

Shivers had been right about the trench in front of the C.P. The Marines could not get out of the command bunker. The Chicom grenades hit the wall of the bunker and fell into the trench, exploding in the entranceway. Although every Marine in the bunker was wounded, they maintained their fire and kept the VC from overrunning the bunker.

"The first thing I knew, one of the PFs yelled 'Boo coo VC,' and before I could roll out of the rack, an RPG hit the bunker," said Lieutenant McDonnell. "Rock jumped out of the top of the bunker—right through the screen. The rest of us got below but we couldn't get outside. Every time someone tried, a Chicom would go off blowing him back inside." Chicoms were Chinese Communist grenades, and although they had plenty of concussion, they lacked the destruction of U.S. fragmentation grenades.

"We could hear Rock yelling outside but we couldn't get out," McDonnell said. "We didn't get anybody killed though. The VC left eight men in the wire, and the people in the ville told us they counted eighteen bodies being carried off, some of them on poles. When they tie a man to a pole, he's dead."

"Rock lost an eye," Shivers said. "He was the most seriously wounded. But he said he was staying in the Corps. It was his left eye, and he can still shoot a rifle."

I asked about the relief force, the legendary company of Marines at Baldy that were to come barreling down the road if the C.P. was under attack.

"They didn't have time," McDonnell said. "And they would have to come right down that road. It would be mined, and they would be very vulnerable to ambush."

"CUPP 4 could see we were under attack," Shivers said, "but they couldn't do anything. They couldn't leave the ville unprotected."

The safety of the C.P. was another illusion I surrendered. I wondered how I would have reacted if I had been there. I couldn't imagine charging the door in the face of grenades and rifle fire. I imagine I would have cowered behind the radio operator, who had reported, "Be advised Third Platoon C.P. under heavy attack. VC inside the wire."

I confess to another thought. In hindsight, knowing that no one who remained in the bunker had been seriously injured, I would like to have been there. I think I would like to know what I would have discovered about myself. And what a story it would have been if I had been there and had found the words and honesty to tell it.

The Golf 2 jeep, a rattling, smoking wreck, came along, driven by a downy-faced, lost-looking PFC who talked to it in personal terms. "All right, you son of a bitch, die on me." Hinkle and I climbed in, and after much swearing and grinding of gears, the driver was able to get the jeep in motion, and we bumped along the dirt roads of Baldy, which were ankle deep in mud or dust, depending on whether it was raining, and along QL 1 toward My Hat and eventually Da Nang.

The driver stopped once to deliver a machine-gun barrel to a lone Marine from CUPP 6 who was waiting for it and then pulled off the highway just short of the Ba Ren bridge at the Golf 2 C.P.

Unlike the Golf 3 C.P., Golf 2 had no view. The command bunker, of single level, was below the highway and the bridge and not much above the water in the river. Inside it was just as dark, airless, and crowded, and perhaps more humid. Lieutenant Smith, who had taken over Second Platoon, greeted us in his unhappy manner.

"Did you go to the hospital to see Rock?" he asked.

"No," I confessed, confirming his view that I, and by extension the rest of the media, was interested in the story not the men. "How is he?"

"I saw him yesterday," Smith said.

I was startled that the lieutenant had been in Da Nang the day before. My trip from Da Nang had taken less than half an hour by helicopter and less than two hours by jeep, yet Da Nang was beyond the imagination of the grunts in Golf CUPP. Most would see it only on arrival and departure; a lucky few would get in-country R and R at China Beach. One of the jarring, unsettling things about Vietnam was the unreality of distance and time. When Rock was wounded in the attack on the Golf 3 C.P., Baldy had seemed a lifetime away. Yet, only yesterday Lieutenant Smith had gone to Da Nang.

"Rock was in good spirits," Smith continued. "He said he was staying in. I think they'll let him; he can still shoot a rifle."

"Were you at the C.P. when it was hit?" I asked.

"No. I had just moved over here. I'll brief you on tomorrow's operation. Every CUPP team has at least one patrol a day in its area of operation plus a night Alley Cat. Two or three times a week we have an operation in the VC sanctuaries. This is usually a sweep or an extended patrol. Tomorrow we will be patrolling outside our area of operation, and we'll be clearing the area of booby traps. The whole area is covered with mines and booby traps. They've got something in there they don't want us to find."

I was disconcerted to find the Marines were going to be looking for booby traps instead of Viet Cong; there was something terrifyingly impersonal about booby traps. Maybe being killed by a man similar to oneself was not heroic, but being killed by a concealed explosive was obscene. There was even an element of shame to it. That's why they were called "booby traps." The victim triggered his own destruction, and his last impulse was hatred toward himself. "Booby!" his mind screamed.

That was for the lucky ones. The unlucky ones lived after "traumatic amputation"—which was a polite term for violent loss of legs, arms, bowels, testicles, eyes. They lived with scarred, mangled bodies and the vivid memory of one moment's carelessness.

In addition to being frightened, I was disheartened; there wasn't much of a story in finding and destroying booby traps. There was no victory, no triumph, only a reprieve. I would have declined the invitation if I could have done so without confirming Smith's opinion that I wasn't really interested in his men but only in headline-grabbing spectacles.

Lieutenant Waldrop had taken the precaution of sending me through the mine school at the Marble Mountain Marine base. The Marines were justly proud of the school. Every time a new type of booby trap was found in the field, the information was sent to the school, and the next day it was included in the curriculum. Four hundred Marines a month went through the school, and fifteen hundred more were trained in the field. The results were evident. In August the Marines found 55 percent of the mines and accidentally detonated 45 percent of them. In December they found 85 percent of them and unintentionally detonated only 15 percent.

"While in the field there is no substitute for alertness, caution, and a suspicious nature," Sgt. Bruce Horn had told me. Horn, one of the instructors at the mine school, had watched me step on the demonstration mines and blunder into the booby traps. Triggering one of the mines brought a recorded explosion and a shouted warning from Horn, "You are dead. You are fucking dead."

Seeing no honorable way out of the operation, I resolved to stay in the middle of the column and to step only in the tracks of the man ahead of me. One of the Marines had to be first in the column. The others had to watch for snipers and ambush and to investigate anything suspicious; I did not.

Lieutenant Smith was going with CUPP 8. I decided to go with CUPP 10 mainly because CUPP 10 lived in the village of Thanh Binh adjacent to the bridge and across the highway from the C.P. A runner came from CUPP 10 to pick up some rations, so Hinkle and I followed him across the highway and through the ville.

Thanh Binh was the area market. The village was dominated by the market — a large open square surrounded by masonry buildings. Every building was marked and scarred by a sapper attack the previous summer. The CUPP team protecting Thanh Binh had been pinned down in its night position by a superior VC force outside the ville, and after mortaring Thanh Binh, VC sappers went through the hamlet throwing satchel charges in the hootches and bunkers. A hundred men, women, and children were killed, and more than eighty wounded. The specter of Thanh Binh hung over the CUPP program. The Marines swore it would never happen again.

We walked through the wide muddy avenue of the now-empty marketplace. Puddles of water stood everywhere. Once past the marketplace, the avenue narrowed to a cart-wide street which had been churned into a quagmire, and then the street played out entirely, and we slipped and skidded along a muddy footpath until we reached the rest of the team sitting in thatch hootches at the edge of the ville. One man came over to greet us. "I'm the doc," he said. "What's your name?"

I gave him my name and my hand, warming to his greeting. None of the others acknowledged our presence. "What's your blood type?" he asked. "What's your zap number?" He wrote down the information in his notebook for future reference and, having lost interest in us, went back to the hootch in which he had been resting.

"The friendly neighborhood corpsman," Hinkle said.

Every Marine, no matter what his military specialty, was expected to be at heart a rifleman. When needed, he was expected to drop his tuba, skillet, typewriter, or truck and grab his rifle. Support services such as chaplains, doctors, and nurses were supplied by the Navy.

Navy hospital corpsmen attached to Marine units were regarded with disdain because they were, after all, Navy. And with respect because, when trouble came, the friendly neighborhood corpsman was in the thick of it, fighting alongside the others and caring for the wounded.

"When the shooting starts I'm as much a Marine as they are," Truhe said.

Hospital Corpsman Third Class Michael Truhe, of Topeka, Kansas, was something unique in Golf Company. A draftee. Having completed his premed training, he was supposed to have filed for another deferment. "I got invited to watch this operation, so I did that instead. After they drafted me, I asked for the Air Force, so they sent me to the Navy. I asked for hospital duty, so they sent me here," Truhe said, gesturing at the mud-floored hootch.

"It don't mean nothing though. I skated for seven months. I was aboard a ship. The first month I was here I treated 396 civilians. Jungle rot, snake bite, gangrene. There are a lot of poisonous snakes here. I had one snakebite victim die, and I called a medevac for another one. He was already in convulsions and he died too. And gangrene. They get a cut and get out in the rice paddies and it gets infected. I used to give mothers medicine and bandages for their kids and show them how to use it so they didn't have to bring the sick kids to me every time, but we recaptured it from the VC, so now I make them bring the kids to me.

"A lot of civilians get hurt with booby traps too. You can tell by the wounds that some of them were setting the booby trap when it went off. We had one whole family hit by a mine. Mamasan, papasan, babysans—they were all squatting down setting this mine and it went off.

"But they were from another ville. This is the most progovernment ville in Vietnam. After the VC attacked this place last summer, the people won't have anything to do with them. If they see something, they tell us. But they're scared. They're afraid the VC will come back. That's why we spend the night in the ville. They won't stay here unless we do. The VC slips in here at night and puts up posters giving our name and a price on our heads, but it don't mean nothing.

"They're going to hit us pretty soon. We haven't been attacked in a long time. They've hit every team in the platoon but us. But it don't mean nothing."

Truhe's conversation was heavily laced with "It don't mean nothing" and "Is that right?" By changing the emphasis on the phrases and stretching *that* into three syllables, the stocky, dark-haired corpsman could use it to express anything from the joy of receiving a letter from his wife with a picture of his baby daughter, to disbelief concerning an order, to despair over bad news regarding one of his patients. "Is thaaat right?" Truhe responded when Sgt. William Dignam came along passing the word that the team was moving.

CUPP 10 moved its position frequently, both to keep an eye on the ville and to let the villagers know they were there. They were also determined that the VC not pin them down in one position where they could not defend the ville. The Marines picked up their heavy packs and slopped through slick mudholes that had once been footpaths to the other side of the hamlet. Sergeant Dignam indicated the hootches into which to place their gear.

Sergeant Dignam was only a couple of years older than the other members of the team and he was humorously laconic, but he had a weight about him, an undercurrent of gravity, that no one else on the team had. "Dig," as he preferred to be called even by officers and PFs, was a veteran of some of the worst fighting in Vietnam. In Operation Union he had been the only member of Delta Company who was not killed or wounded when they had been ambushed in the mountains. He had also been at Khe Sahn and in the battle of Hue.

Dig, who was tall and lanky, had a way of smiling when he spoke, as though he were laughing at himself, amused that he was still alive. "This platoon has never rotated a man," he said. "Every one of them has been a medevac or permanent routine. 'Permanent routine' is what you call when a man is dead, to let the helicopters know there is no hurry about picking him up. Ortega will be the first man in Second Platoon ever to rotate."

"It don't mean nothing," said Truhe.

Corporal Ortega, from Houston, Texas, said nothing. The tall, nonchalant Ortega spent a lot of time to himself, and when he was with others, he usually played the clown.

I stepped into one of the hootches and was snapped at by a dog. The identification 7K33 was tattooed in the dog's ear, and he responded to the name *Russell*. "Don't worry if he bites you, he's had his shots," said the dog handler, Cpl. Daniel Phillips of Ridgecrest, California. "It's that doggie uniform you're wearing." I was wearing Army fatigues instead of the camouflage utilities the Marines wore. "He doesn't like that uniform, but he won't bother anyone wearing one of these tree suits. Sit down and let him get used to you, and he won't snap at you anymore."

Sitting down beside the huge black dog was not easy to do, even though the handler held him and spoke soothingly to him. "Russ bit a kid this morning," he said. "I told them to stay away from him, that he bites, but they've never seen a dog like this, and they kept running up and teasing him, and Russ grabbed one of them. Luckily I was right there and I yelled at him and he let go. Russ is a good dog. He had her down though. Doc put a bandage on her. Russ has had all his shots. I mean, she won't get rabies or anything. It's not like being bitten by one of these Vietnamese dogs. Man, if one of them bites you, they start giving you shots before they bandage the wound.

"The PFs got all excited about the girl being bitten. One of them pointed his rifle at Russ, and I thumbed my M-16 to full automatic and pointed it at him. If he had shot Russ I would have killed him. I mean, I'm sorry as hell about the little girl, but these dogs save a lot of lives and I'm responsible for him. The PFs leave the dogs alone, but the kids think they can play with them."

Phillips cradled Russ's head and scratched his ears. "Correction is more important than affection in training these dogs," he said. "You have to discipline them. You have to punish them when they mess up. But you get tight with the dogs. Hell, your life depends on them."

Phillips became thoughtful as he sat and patted the dog. Like most of the dog handlers, he was concerned about what would happen to the dogs when the Americans left. And already they were leaving. "I'll buy Russ if they'll let me," he said. "I can't see leaving these dogs here for the ARVN. If they get hungry, they'll eat them. I'll turn Russ loose before I'll let the ARVN have him. They'll kill him, but at least he'll have a chance. I think when the Americans leave they ought to take the dogs with them. Some of these dogs have been over here for three years."

The Marines talked about another dog, a small Vietnamese dog that had slipped into one of the hootches and eaten some Composition Four, a plastic explosive.

"He ran outside, kicked about three times, and was dead," Dig said.

"He hadn't even stopped kicking when some Vietnamese ran out and grabbed him. They were going to eat him," Ortega said.

"Doc" Truhe was asked whether or not the explosive would have any effect on the humans who ate the dog. He was of the opinion that it would not, since the dog had not lived long enough to assimilate the explosive.

At dusk the Marines picked up their gear and we moved again, splashing and slipping in the mudholes until we reached the marketplace in the center of the ville. The marketplace was a kind of square, and the masonry houses on the square had high, wide concrete walkways where merchandise was displayed during the day. Wordlessly the Marines scattered out along the square, picking a place and unrolling their poncho and poncho liner for a pillow, and slept with their rifles at their side. The walkways were roofed over with tin, but the tin had been sieved with shrapnel. A slight mist was falling, and the moisture collected on the roof and dripped through the holes.

Dig went about setting up watches for the night, and Truhe made his position known in case he should be needed before morning. Some of the Marines lay down to rest. Others, mostly those who were going on the ambush, sat in groups of two or three smoking and talking quietly. Hinkle had just gotten his private flying license before leaving the States. Another, a redheaded corporal, had a commercial license plus a helicopter rating.

"You could be flying over here," said Hinkle.

"Naw, I would have had to sign up for another year."

"You're crazy. You could be in the air wing. That's better than being on the ground, even if you did have to stay in an extra year."

"I wanted to know what it was like on the ground," said the redhead. "You see more."

He picked up the M-60 machine gun when Dig came along forming the ambush. The ville was totally black as Dig placed the PFs between the Marines and led the way along the muddy street and then on the footpaths. Hinkle and I went with them. I had never experienced such darkness. It was impossible to see the footpath, and men slipped and fell, dropping their rifles in the muck. We passed between hootches, through a gap in a barbed-wire fence that kept cows out of the ville, and then around the outskirts of the hamlet. Dig placed the men to cover an expanse of open rice paddy and to flank a treeline that grew right to the edge of the ville. The PFs whispered a little, moved around to find a comfortable position on the muddy ground, and then became quiet.

Time passed slowly. An occasional flare threw shadows across the rice fields. The mosquitoes buzzed, and it was hard to refrain from slapping at them, but the sound of a slap carried easily in the night air. The night was so quiet that any movement, a man shifting his weight from one haunch to another, drew attention. After staring at the darkness for a while, even the trees seemed to move.

Without warning, it began to rain steadily, almost silently. The PFs got up and began moving around. Dig came along forming up the men for the walk back to the ville. The Marines moved quietly on the way back, watching the hootches, crossing open areas one man at a time. When a falling man made a muffled splash, the file paused for a moment to keep the proper interval. When we reached the square, the Marines headed for their bedrolls and the relative shelter of the perforated roof.

"When it starts raining the PFs want to come in," Dig said. "You can make them stay, but they'll move around and give away your position, or they'll pretend they see something and start shooting. After they've busted your ambush, you have to come in."

I placed my poncho and liner where it would miss most of the drips from the roof, rolled up in it, and with my helmet for a pillow and flak jacket to soften the concrete under my shoulders, tried to sleep. I was still awake when a man came to awaken Truhe for the next watch. The Marine tapped Truhe on the shoulder, and Truhe rolled over with a cocked U.S. Army Model 1911AI Colt .45 in the man's face. The Marine backed up. "Don't touch me when I'm asleep," Truhe said. "All a man has to do is whisper 'Doc' and it wakes me up."

The Marines moved again before daylight. "Get your gear together, we've moving out," Dig said. In a couple of minutes the team and the PFs were in the street, and we walked through the dark, sleeping village and into some hootches to wait for daylight. As soon as day began to break, we lighted heat tabs to boil water for coffee and the freeze-dried Long Range Patrol rations. We would be on the move at first light.

Everywhere we had gone, the team had carried along a large box or locker with the gear in it—flares, extra ammo, grenades. Dig went through the box taking out flares and smoke grenades, which he passed out to the men to carry. He announced it was time to go; the radio operator reported that we were Oscar Mike, and we filed out of the hootch and walked along the same slippery footpath that we had followed to the ambush site the previous night. Now we could see the mudholes and tried to jump over or step around them. Not everyone succeeded.

We passed through the barbed-wire gap. Outside the ville there was better footing and Dig organized the patrol. There would be two dogs and handlers, and they would rotate on the point. The PFs were alternated between the Marines. I was to stay between my escort, Hinkle, and Doc Truhe, who was always in the center of the column. The center was the safest place, and it permitted Truhe to reach any casualties rapidly.

"Aren't you going?" Dig asked Ortega, who was still standing nonchalantly, although the front of the column had started to move. Dig, at twenty-four, was the oldest of the CUPP team leaders. As sergeant, he also held the highest rank, as the others were corporals. But there was another difference. Some fire had been burned out of Dig in that ambush of Delta Company, and what was left was an almost oriental patience. I never heard Dig give a direct order.

"Oh, am I going?" Ortega asked innocently. He picked up his rifle and waded through the paddy, passing the slow-moving file on the paddy dike to take his place behind the dog handlers.

"When he goes, Ortega always walks point," Truhe said. "He's got a sixth sense. Once he stopped because he felt something was wrong. Two PFs walked past him, and the second one hit a 105 booby trap. He was dead when he hit the ground, and a piece of it hit the first PF in the back. It just opened up his whole back as neat as a scalpel. The fragment was so hot it fused two of his vertebrae together. Man, was he in pain. He was screaming and pissing and crapping in his pants. He lived, but he was paralyzed from the waist. Booby traps really mess a man up, and when that happens, the PFs want to go home."

The PFs weren't alone. I wanted to go home too.

We came to a cut in the paddy dike where water could run from one field into another. Those at the front of the column had stepped or jumped across it, but in doing so their boots had chewed up the dike, so that it was necessary for the rest of us to step into the water. Progress was slow, as the dog handlers moved with caution. "This area is bad," Truhe said. "It's so bad Lieutenant Smith said we didn't have to go out without dogs."

Soon we came to a wider cut in the dike, and this time everyone had to wade. The water was knee deep and the mud so sticky that I had to balance my weight on one foot and forcibly jerk the other free. Several men lost their balance and fell into the water. On the other side of the water the dike was narrower and churned so by boots that it required concentration and balance not to slip off the dike and into the paddy. Concentrating on footing meant less alertness to mines, snipers, and ambush.

CUPP 8 joined the end of the column. After a couple of hundred meters we came to a swift, crotch-deep stream which had to be waded. The bank was high and steep, and each man held out his rifle to the man behind to help him up the bank. Once past the stream we were out of the rice field and in an uncultivated area of low weeds bordered by treelines. CUPP 10 followed a dim path through the weeds. CUPP 8 split off to circle around the left flank.

The command helicopter carrying Lieutenant Hess hovered

over the treelines, the rotor wash blowing the trees apart while the door gunners looked for hidden trenches or bunkers. From the ground the helicopter seemed several times to disappear into the trees.

The chopper pilot asked CUPP 10 to pop a green flare to identify itself. Dig called for a flare from the Marine to whom he had given them. "I left them with my pack," said the Marine, who was new to the team. "I didn't think we'd need flares in the daytime." Dig found that the radioman was carrying a white flare, so he popped that.

The dogs discovered some object almost totally buried in the ground, and the column stopped while the handlers scratched around the ground trying to discover what had alerted the dogs. They couldn't find a booby trap, but they passed the word to avoid the object anyway. As the column passed, we all eyed the object suspiciously—a hollow, pipelike metal object which barely protruded above the ground.

Lieutenant Smith radioed for CUPP 10 to pop a flare so CUPP 8 could get a fix on their position. It was important for the two units to know one another's position to avoid shooting each other if the enemy popped up between them. Dig called for another flare but no one had one. He popped a smoke grenade instead, but because of the thick treelines between the two teams, CUPP 8 could not see it.

Smith, the "Golf 3 Actual," called Dig, the "CUPP 10 Actual," to the radio and told him, "If you ever come out here again without flares, you'll regret it."

Dig did not try to pass the blame to the PFC who had left the flares. Dig, who had been a survivor in one of the worst ambushes in the war, was beyond such things.

"See that?" Truhe asked, pointing out a brushy, weed-covered area. "That used to be a ville." By looking, it was possible to find the remains of pounded-earth floors and the circular Buddhist graves that had been overgrown with weeds and almost obliterated by the rains. "I don't know how long it's been gone, but no one that's in the team now ever saw it. But if we get pinned down here, we can't get artillery support because it's marked on the maps as a 'friendly overlay.'"

"We can get support from the Korean artillery faster than we can from our own. They don't mess around with clearances," said another Marine.

A ROK Marine division flanked the Fifth Marine position. Like most of the U.S. Marines, CUPP 10 Marines had a high opinion of the Korean Marines. "Man, they are squared away. They have their shit wired," the U.S. Marines said. The respect was mutual. The ROK Marines had been trained by and patterned after their U.S. counterparts, and they referred to the Americans as "our brother Marines."

"You know what I think we ought to do with this country," said the redheaded Marine who wanted to see what the war looked like from the ground. "I think we ought to turn it over to the Koreans. In four years they would have this country squared away."

Such an attitude might be surprising to men who served in Korea in the early days of that war, but while I never met a Marine in Vietnam who thought another outfit was superior to his own, many of them admitted that the superbly disciplined and conditioned ROK Marines were just as good.

We had been standing for some time in what appeared to be an abandoned cane field. The word was passed that the point had discovered a bunker and that we were to move up carefully, as the area was mined. We kept walking forward until the team was squeezed into a little clearing surrounded by a profusion of trees. To the right was a large bunker with a right-angled opening that made it impossible to see or fire into it. To our front was the river, which was hidden behind trees. A trail ran parallel to the river, and Marines had moved a short distance both ways. The dog handlers warned them not to go far, as the path had not been swept. Between the bunker and the river was a freshly dug mound of dirt with a rusty flare protruding from it. The dog handlers warned everyone to stay away from it.

"This is our blocking position," Dig said. "Make yourself comfortable."

The men sat down, first finding a piece of clear, unmarked ground, then squatting and examining it closely and slowly sitting down on it. Truhe stepped on a buried rusted can that gave under his weight. He swore, thinking he had triggered a mine. "Is that right?" he said, whistling softly. "I felt something give under my foot, and I thought it was the plunger on a mine."

Ortega walked back and forth along the footpath, looking first one way and then the other, and checking along the tree-lined river bank for hiding VC. He clicked the safety off his M-16. "Any PFs down that way?" he asked.

"Any PFs down that way?" Dig asked the PF honcho. "No PFs."

"I just saw a man with a rifle. He was wearing a green uniform and had a towel around his neck," Ortega said.

"No PF," the honcho said. "NVA." However, the man had already disappeared in the thick foliage. The radio operator called CUPP 8 to advise them that a man had been seen coming down the path and was now headed in their direction.

"Gook," the PF honcho said.

Although many Americans referred to all Vietnamese, indeed all Orientals as gooks, the CUPP Marines used *gook* as synonymous with Viet Cong, and the PFs used the word the same way.

An explosion went off in distance, and several of the Marines jumped and swore. "Is thaat riiight?" Truhe said. The CUPP 8 leader called to advise that a PF had just triggered a booby trap and that they were calling for a medevac. "What happened to the dog?" one of the handlers asked. Unlike CUPP 10, CUPP 8 had only one dog. "The PF wandered off the trail," the radio operator reported.

"You hear that," Dig said to the PF honcho. "Don't let your men go wandering around."

The warning was too late however. One PF was already crawling into the bunker. "Get out of there," some of the Marines called. Others got up and moved away from the bunker.

The PF crawled partway into the bunker, apparently thought better of it, and backed out. The PF honcho went over to the bunker and began poking the outside with a stick. He called Dig over and showed him a rice cache buried at the side of the bunker. "We'll blow it when we leave," Dig said.

I had taken off the hot, heavy steel helmet when I sat on the ground, but with all the moving around, I put it back on and zipped up my flak jacket. This drew comments from some of the Marines who were not wearing helmets but camouflage bush hats.

"Just do what the corpsman does," Truhe said. "You'll never

see a corpsman out here without his helmet and flak jacket. He's seen too many head wounds."

"That helmet won't stop much," Dig said.

"You know what it takes to kill you?" Truhe asked. "A piece of metal about the size of a pinhead. That's all it takes. A helmet doesn't have to stop much. I'll wear one for a year if it'll stop just one piece of metal from hitting me in the brain."

There was another explosion. "CUPP 8, CUPP 8, CUPP 10," the radio operator called. "What is your situation?" For a moment he held the phone to his ear. "The dog tripped an 81mm booby trap," he reported to Dig. "It was a dud. They just destroyed it."

There were whistles and exclamations and questions as to who the hell was the dog handler. Both the dog handlers with CUPP 10 came to the dog's defense. "The dog is tired," they explained. "He's been going a long time. A dog can work for only about forty-five minutes, and after that he loses his alertness and has to be rested. We were rotating on the point, but that dog has been working the whole time."

There was another explosion, and again the radio operator called CUPP 8. "Request sit rep." (Situation report) "They just found another booby trap and detonated it," he said to Dig. "Keep us informed, CUPP 8," he said into the telephone.

Two PFs, perhaps out of curiosity, perhaps out of bravado, walked behind the bunker and began investigating what appeared to be the ruins of a garden. The trees had been cleared from the plot, but weeds and low bushes had again overgrown it. The Marines watched the PFs with apprehension. "They're going to get blown away," Truhe said.

The two PFs spotted a tube up in a tree and pointed it out. Dig and some of the other Marines had spotted it earlier. They didn't know what it was, but they were unanimous in their advice to leave it alone.

"The dog just tripped another mine. Another dud. This one was a shaped charge," the radio operator said. The shaped charge was a mine designed to spew hundreds of pellets in a cone-shaped pattern down the trail. For a few minutes no one spoke, and then Phillips came to the defense of the dog.

"Dogs are 80 percent effective when they are fresh," he said.

"When they get tired they get careless. It's not always the fault of the dog either. Sometimes the handler fails to read the dog. You have to work with the dog and know how he alerts. Sometimes a dog will step or jump over a trip wire and you have to see him do it."

"There's somebody moving on the other side of the river," Ortega said. Several of the Marines moved into position and waited. Whatever it was, went away. Ortega relaxed.

"There's a sniper over there, and he's going to shoot you right through the back of the head," one Marine said to Ortega. The Marines spent the next few minutes describing in gory detail how each was going to die and reliving the close calls they had had and how scared they had been. It was a rough brand of humor, but it passed the time and seemed to relieve tension.

"Not me," said Dig, when the others talked of their fear. "I was one of 'Delta's Walking Dead.'" "The Walking Dead of Delta" were the nine men from Delta Company who survived the ambush. When they were rescued, only Dig was still able to fire a weapon. "If they didn't get me at Union or Hue, they aren't going to get me out here."

"Union was rough, wasn't it?" someone asked.

"There was no cover," Dig said. "You just stuck your bayonet in the ground and hid behind it."

"You know, this platoon has never rotated a man," Truhe said. "Ortega will be the first. But there hasn't been a Marine killed since I've been here."

"Man, look at that," said the redheaded pilot, pointing at the sky. It was the Freedom Bird carrying a full load of GIs back to the States.

"I'm a draftee," said Truhe. "I've got a little girl I've never seen. But if they ever shoot at the Freedom Bird, I swear I'll extend. I believe if the gooks ever shot down one of those, every man over here would extend to get the guy who did it."

CUPP 8 called, wanting to know CUPP 10's position. They were of the opinion that they had walked far enough to reach CUPP 10. "Wait one," the radio operator called. Dig and some of the other Marines got out a map and compass and plotted their position. After several checks, Dig decided that CUPP 10 was exactly where it was supposed to be, and he told the radio operator to pass the information to CUPP 8.

"Lieutenant Smith is unhappy with you because you didn't bring any flares to mark our position," the radio operator told Dig.

"I'm not lost," Dig said. "He's the one who's lost."

Truhe went over to try his hand at the map and compass, and after he had tried it, others did the same. There was some argument, but the consensus of opinion was that CUPP 10 was in its proper position and was blocking the trail.

"Stand by," the radio operator said. "CUPP 8 just found a bunker complex and a booby-trap factory, and they are going to blow it. Lieutenant Smith wants you to listen and take a compass bearing on the explosion."

Dig drew a lot of advice and company as he listened for the explosion and tried to determine a compass bearing on it. There was some disagreement about the exact direction from which the sound came, but Dig got a reading and reported it. Lieutenant Smith asked if they could hear CUPP 8 coming down the trail. Ortega went down the trail a short way and listened but could hear nothing. There was another heated radio exchange as Lieutenant Smith decided that CUPP 10 was not in a position to block the trail that CUPP 8 was clearing.

Some PFs went down the trail to listen also. "Get those PFs out of there," Dig told the PF honcho. "CUPP 8 will see them and start shooting."

Lieutenant Smith called, asking Dig to fire a few rounds in the air so CUPP 8 could tell how close they were. Dig did so, and then CUPP 8 fired a few rounds in return. Dig called to tell Lieutenant Smith that they were close by and that there was a trail near the river. However, CUPP 8 was not on the river. CUPP 8 was following a heavily booby-trapped trail which was overgrown with brush and grass, and the two trails did not intersect. Although on the map the two teams appeared to be close, the impenetrable vegetation turned that short distance into a couple of hours of hard chopping to break through to each other. Lieutenant Smith told CUPP 10 that they might as well go back to the ville, as they were not blocking the right trail.

Dig started the patrol out of the clearing, leaving two men behind to blow up the bunker and rice cache. "Fire in the hole," the two men yelled as they came running down the trail. The bunker made only a muffled noise as it blew, but the rice went up in a high column of dust and smoke.

"Is that right?" Truhe said. "There was a pressure mine under the rice." A booby trap had been placed under the rice cache to detonate when the rice was disturbed.

"We'll get hit going back to the ville," Truhe said. "That's when we always get hit, when we're going back."

"If they hit me they'll have to hit a moving target," said the redhead, in a joke that was almost as old as war itself.

We moved back through the tree-lined, uncultivated area, and once the patrol reached the rice paddies, the formation was lost as the Marines and PFs struck out on their own for the ville.

The villagers stood in the doorways of their hootches to watch as CUPP 10 passed back through the ville. Many of them were watching out of curiosity, but some of them were families waiting for the PF husband and father to come home. Some of the PFs had cut stalks of sugarcane for their children. A small dog ran out of one of the hootches to bark at Russ, but Phillips held Russ on a tight leash. The Vietnamese got out of the dog's way.

We went into the hootches the team would occupy for its day position, and the Marines began peeling off their muddy boots and socks. Some of the men pulled off their trousers, but most just scraped off the mud and left them on to dry. Phillips came in the hootch, and Russell jumped up on a plank bed before an altar. "That's number ten," Truhe said. "You have to keep that dog away from the altar."

Phillips moved the dog, and just as he did, a young Vietnamese boy came running through the door. Russ snapped at the child, but Daniel pulled the dog back. "You know better than that," Dig said, calling the child by name. "Don't you run up to that dog. You come in the other door." The boy went around the hootch to a door on the other side.

It was a large hootch with a flimsy partition across the middle. The Marines were on one side, a Vietnamese family on the other. The little boy came through the partition looking for the dog, and the Marines gave him money to buy them some Cokes and French bread to have with their C rations. The soft drinks were warm; the bread was fresh and delicious.

"This bread is the best thing they have over here," Truhe said, digging in his pockets for more piasters.

"There goes CUPP 8," someone said, and we watched out of the open door of the hootch as the tired, bedraggled Marines slipped along the muddy footpath. "Lieutenant Smith looks real unhappy."

"Are you going to report?" someone asked Dig.

"He knows I'm here," Dig said. Actually Dig had decided to wait until Lieutenant Smith had time to eat and get cleaned up. Also, Phillips was taking Russell back to the rear for more training, and the dog handler wanted to wash the muddy dog before leaving. Dig decided to wait for him.

There was a well just off the muddy narrow street that led to the square. Already it was surrounded by Marines who were trying to wash the mud off their boots and trousers. Phillips dipped out water with his helmet and threw it on the dog and squeezed off most of the mud. The street in front of the well was a quagmire, and to keep the dog clean, Phillips decided to carry the dog across it. However, his feet slipped, and he and the dog fell sprawling in the mud.

We waited for Phillips to wash the dog again and walked to the C.P. Phillips and I waited outside while Dig made his report. Phillips tied the dog outside the PF bunker because three little girls kept running past the front of the dog to see him snap. Also, Russ was tempted by the Hondas that passed along the highway. After a few mintues the PF honcho came out and asked Phillips to move the dog. There were two PFs in the bunker, and they were afraid to come out while the dog was there.

Dig came out, unperturbed as usual. "Did Lieutenant Smith give you a hard time?" I asked.

"No, he just said we needed better coordination. No one knew there were two trails in there," Dig said. "Actually he was pleased about finding that booby-trap factory, and he wouldn't have found it if he had been on the right trail. That'll slow them down for a while."

The dog handler who had been with CUPP 8 came out of the C.P. and walked down to the river. He had a can of beer in his hand but was just holding it and staring at the river. Phillips walked down to talk to him. I followed.

"I'm not going out with that dog again," the handler said quietly. "He tripped three booby traps, and they were all three duds. I had a dog before, a good one. But I'm not going with this one again."

"What'll happen to the dog?" Phillips asked.

"I don't care. I don't have to go out with a dog I don't trust. They can give him to the ARVN for all I care." He stared at the water without seeming to see the debris and dead fish that floated there. He seemed to have forgotten the can of beer in his hand. "I'm going back to the rear," he said.

A few days later I was back at Baldy, this time for an island operation. There was something about the words *island operation* that brought visions of Iwo Jima and Guadalcanal, of landing craft crawling through the surf and green-clad Marines charging across the beaches and into the trees. This island operation was going to be different. We were waiting on the bridge for helicopters to lift us to the island.

There were a lot of people at Baldy—reporters, photographers, television crews—drawn by the mystique surrounding Marines and island operations. First, we had pillaged the Marine Public Affairs Office for helmets, canteens, packs, flak jackets, ponchos, and liners.

After a helicopter trip to Baldy, we were taken to the Golf Operations Center to be briefed by Captain Tilley. Tilley had just returned from R and R in Hawaii with his wife, and like most men returning from vacation he felt a letdown that the respite was over and a reluctance to get back into the work routine. Tilley was frustrated in his need to grab the reins of command and get everything squared away with a dozen correspondents underfoot.

Leaving us standing outside, Lieutenant Waldrop from the PAO office went inside to inform Captain Tilley that a dozen extra men were going along on the assault. We couldn't hear what the soft-voiced Waldrop was saying, but we could hear Tilley, the counterpuncher. "God dammit, I'm trying to fight a war."

"Another one of those," one of the television crewmen said, and we exchanged knowing looks. After a few minutes Tilley appeared at the door and reluctantly invited us in.

We crowded into the operations center, filling up the hastily arranged benches and chairs, so that the last men in had to stand. Tilley stood before a detailed map and outlined Golf Company's area of responsibility. He explained the Combined Unit Pacification Program, the Marines' personal involvement with the people in the villes, and told of the PF school, the gardens, the experimental pig farm, and the building of pagodas, schools, and council houses. "Any questions?" he asked.

"How many cases of rape have you had?" Produce and pacification were not news.

"There has never been a charge of assault against a CUPP Marine," Tilley said. "Or molesting or stealing."

"I understand marijuana grows wild here. Do you have any trouble with Marines on pot or hard drugs?"

Tilley replied that there had been no trouble with drugs among the CUPP Marines. One Marine was being discharged because he had been caught with marijuana in his possession; however, he was with headquarters and not a CUPP team.

"We hear of instances where men have refused to go on patrol unless they understand the reason for it. Is that a problem here?"

Tilley said that his men knew what they were there for and that there had been no instances where a man had questioned the need for a patrol or had refused to go on one. "The problem here is that every time there is an operation, every cook and clerk wants to go."

"There have been a lot of fragging stories where enlisted men have attacked their officers. Has that ever happened here?"

"If you want to know how my men feel about me, ask them," Tilley said, and turning the rest of the briefing over to Lieutenant Hess, he left.

Tilley felt that he had been insulted, along with the men of his company and the uniform he wore. But the reporters had intended no insult. They were just after a story, and it was hard to write an incisive, headline-grabbing story about Marines teaching Vietnamese farmers to grow cabbage. They didn't pass out Pulitzers for that. Marines were news when they were killing or being killed. Raising a rifle or a flag, yes; raising watermelons or a school, no.

I had seen more drugs on a college campus than I saw in Vietnam. However, a student smoking pot was neither a scandal nor news. A Marine smoking pot was both. And in the news equation one Marine with marijuana in his possession was more important than ten gardens, a school, and an experimental pig farm.

Like the others, I had come to see a battle, not a garden, and I felt the ambivalence known to most reporters. I didn't want anything bad to happen to these men. I really didn't. In my esteem they stood far above most young men of their age. But a disaster, a tragedy, would make a great story, and if one happened I wanted to be there. In Vietnam, as in America, good news was no news.

The grunts knew why we were there, but rather than animosity, there was a desire to be helpful to us. In addition to self-conscious quotations, they tried to make stories for us, and in front of the cameras, particularly the television cameras, there was a self-conscious bravado. It was important to them that what was happening be reported. It was important that they be noticed, that they be seen.

Lieutenant Hess pointed out the island on the map. It was an island in the river, not a movie-real island at all. The VC used it for a rest camp. The Marines had assaulted the island three times and had caught the enemy on the island each time. "I don't know why, but they continue to use it. Our information is that there are VC on the island again."

The island was heavily wooded, but there was a clearing at one end where helicopters could land. The operation itself would be conducted by Vietnamese Regional Forces with Lieutenant Smith as adviser, and one Marine radio operator with each helicopter as liaison. I think all of us blanched at this. Regional Forces, or RFs, were considered to be little better than PFs and much inferior to regular ARVN units. However, the Marines had a high regard for this RF unit, and the correspondents decided to go on the assault itself, landing with the RFs rather than with the Marine blocking force across the river.

"There may be a problem of space on the helicopters," Lieutenant Hess said. "We do have another operation—a night operation with CUPP 6. It's a small operation, but we usually get a lot of contacts on night ops. However, you will not get back in time for the island operation."

The night operation was of no interest to the photographers and television crews, as they could not use their cameras, and the others believed the larger island operation was more newsworthy. I decided to go on the night operation, as I preferred not to have the company of so many reporters. A *Stars and Stripes* reporter, Sp5c. Steven Kroft, who had done an earlier story on CUPP 6, also decided to go.

I was glad to have Kroft along. He had once asked me to accompany him on a train trip from Da Nang to Hue for a story he wanted to do about the train. Because of its penchant for getting itself blown up or ambushed, the train was off-limits to U.S. military personnel at the time, and Kroft wanted a buddy along.

The train trip had been uneventful, but in Hue we had been attacked by two "Honda Charlies," teenage boys who robbed and sometimes mugged Americans. The driver came up behind us and drove his Honda motorcyle between us. The rider grabbed for our cameras. In a brief tussle they broke Kroft's camera but we got their Honda. I wanted to take the Honda and chase them down, but Kroft advised restraint, as there were strong anti-American feelings in Hue. I had learned to respect Kroft's courage and his judgment.

Lieutenant Hess offered us weapons. I recalled the nakedness I had felt walking through a ville without one. This was going to be an even smaller group, and I could not ask them to protect me. "Yes," I said.

"You want a rifle or pistol?"

"Rifle," I said. I couldn't imagine a pistol being of much use, at least not in my hands.

For the first time Lieutenant Hess looked at me with approval. "You can have Ortega's rifle," he said, handing me an M-16 and a bandoleer of ammo.

I recognized the rifle. Seven notches had been cut in the handgrip, and a red plastic rose was tied to the front sight. When I examined it closer I saw that the handgrip had been chewed up and that there was a hole in the stock. Dried blood was caked on the barrel. "What happened to Ortega?" I asked. Ortega was going to be the first man to rotate from Second Platoon.

"Mine," Hess said. "He'll live but he was messed up."

I took the rifle, although I didn't expect to have to use it. My fear was of accidentally shooting someone. I had noticed more than once a carelessness in handling the automatic rifles and had several times had them pointed at me without malice.

Cpl. Bill Baldwin, who was going as our escort, took the rifle, checked to see that it was operating properly, and cleaned off most of the blood. Lieutenant Hess found a rifle for Kroft, and we left the others at the operations center and were taken by the Golf 2 jeep down the highway to a trail that led through trees and rice paddies to the ville in which CUPP 6 lived. The members of the team were standing beside a hootch listening to Lieutenant Smith. They turned to watch our approach. "These two reporters want to go along on the night op," Corporal Baldwin said.

The Marines showed no enthusiasm for our presence. They looked like boys who had just been told that they would have to take their little sisters on their fishing trip. They could still go, but it wouldn't be the same.

"Roseberry was just going to take a handful of men so they could move fast," Lieutenant Smith said. "If he takes very many the VC will avoid them. But if you go along we'll have to send some extra men to protect you."

Kroft and I could see the problem but we wanted to go. On my part, I had some misgivings about going with a small unit at night, but something obstinate in me wanted to go precisely because they didn't want me along.

"We're going to move fast and hit them hard," said a thin, almost frail Marine. "We're going to take only part of the team and our best two PFs."

The thin, unimpressive-looking Marine was Cpl. Mike Roseberry. Roseberry, who claimed to be twenty, although he looked scarcely sixteen, was the leader of CUPP 6 and was highly regarded by both his men and his superiors.

"Had you rather we not go, Mike?" asked Kroft, who had written a story on Roseberry and CUPP 6. Kroft regarded Roseberry as a hero.

"We'd like to keep it small so we can move fast without much noise," Roseberry said.

Roseberry didn't say it, but if we went along the plans for the operation would have to be changed. But I wanted to go, and I had a premonition that if I didn't, I would miss something.

Kroft took me to one side. "I know Mike," he said. "He won't say anything, but he doesn't want us to go, and I'm not going if he doesn't want us to."

"We can keep up," I told Roseberry.

"It's not a question of keeping up," Roseberry said. He didn't say it, but he didn't want to have to be responsible for a couple of reporters bumbling around at night in dangerous country. It was enough to have to worry about their own lives. Kroft and I were both carrying rifles but we didn't fool anybody.

"Captain Tilley said we could go," I said, playing my trump. Nobody said anything. It was going to be harder than I thought. "If you tell us not to go, we won't go," I said.

There was a general shifting of feet and looking around but no one said anything. Lieutenant Smith was clearly in a quandary. To invite us was to end the operation as it was planned and perhaps ruin its effectiveness. To forbid us was to invite the hostility of the press. There were a lot of scare stories about what had happened to the careers of officers who had offended the press.

"We can't tell you that you can't go," Smith said. "But this operation means a lot to us. I'd hate to see it get messed up."

He didn't say we would mess up the operation, but if something went wrong and someone got hurt, I knew it would be hard for me to live with.

"If we don't go on this, can we still get in on the island operation?" Kroft asked.

Lieutenant Smith guaranteed us a place on a helicopter, and reluctantly we took it.

Smith looked unhappy as he completed his briefing to his troops. He had put his men and his mission first, but he seemed to be wondering if he hadn't put his career second. The men who were going on the operation plainly looked relieved that it would go as planned and without us.

"Be sure you take plenty of morphine," Smith told Corpsman Jim Napier. "If a man is hit, knock him out. You're not going to be able to get a medevac before daylight, and you can't have a man out there screaming and giving away your position."

After the briefing, Lieutenant Smith led us back through the ville and to the highway, where we could catch a jeep to the Golf 2 C.P. "I know you wanted to go," he said apologetically. "But this is important to us. The VC think they own the night around here. They think they can move at will. We're trying to change their minds."

If we had gone along would Roseberry have tried to avoid enemy contact to protect us, or would he have taken additional

risks to provide us with a story? Left unstated was the impli-
cation that the media had the power to change the plans and
perhaps the effectiveness of operations, at least small-unit operations.

When we got back to the Golf 2 C.P. beside the Song Ba Ren,
Smith went off to find places for all the correspondents to sleep.
There was not enough room for everyone. "I'm going to have to
send some of you people over to CUPP 10 to spend the night,
but I'll get them to bring you back at daylight so you can go on
the operation," Lieutenant Smith said.

A wire-service reporter decided to go with Kroft and me to
CUPP 10. Corporal Baldwin was to accompany us as escort. We
waited beside the C.P., and after a while Corpsman Truhe came
along to pick up some rations. "These people are going to spend
the night with you, but they're coming back in the morning in
time to go on the assault," Smith told him.

"By the way, I talked to the Battalion Aid Station, and they
say you saved Ortega's foot. If you had turned it the other way,
he would have lost it. And they found his other nut. It was up
inside him."

"Is thaat right?" Truhe said, clearly excited. "Dig and Ortega
were both hit after you were here," he said to me. "Booby trap.
Dig just got a broken ankle, but Ortega was really messed up.
His foot was just hanging by a shred. But I remembered, turn
it away from the uninjured part. Things like that come back to
you. Now if he doesn't get an infection . . .

"But I was worried about that other testicle. I found one of
them, but he was all messed up, blood everywhere, and I couldn't
find the other one. Ortega kept raising up and trying to look,
and he was screaming, 'My nuts, my nuts.' He was really worried, but I got where he couldn't see around me. I thought he'd
lost it though. I should have remembered—a testicle is on a very
strong cord, and when something like that happens it snaps right
up into the body cavity. He's going to be all right though."

Truhe continued to talk about Ortega as he led us to the
CUPP 10 day pos, past a monument listing the names of the
villagers killed in the VC attack the previous summer. CUPP
10 was sitting beside the ruins of a church destroyed by the VC,
and when Truhe saw the other members of the team, he had to
tell them the good news. "Ortega's going to be OK. If I had turned

his foot the other way, he would have lost it, but they think they can save it now. If he just doesn't get an infection. And they found his other testicle. It was up in his body cavity. See, a testicle is attached to this cord—its so small you can hardly see it—but it's very strong. It's like a rubber band, and when he was hit he just sucked it up inside his body cavity. You know, Ortega used to talk about that all the time. He was really afraid of losing his balls."

"This platoon still hasn't rotated a man," someone said.

The thought sobered Truhe. "That's right. Ortega was going to be the first man to rotate. Wonder who's next on the list?"

Perhaps the men thought of some names, but no one mentioned one.

"It don't mean nothing," someone said, and they dropped the subject.

At dusk we walked along the outskirts of the ville and moved into some hootches. The trails were still muddy, but water was standing in only a few places. I went into a large thatch hootch that had a fragile partition across the middle. In one room was a woman with several young children. She was cooking their supper on a fire laid on the floor. The hootch had no chimney, and the smoke was heavy as it filtered slowly through the thatch roof—but it discouraged mosquitoes. In addition to the fire, there was a crude oil lamp made of a C-ration can. The woman kept pointing at her head and saying something to Truhe. He ignored her.

"Dien cai dau," she said. She was saying there was something "crazy" with her head.

"She says she's got a headache," a Marine explained to Truhe. "She wants something for her head."

"I know what she wants," Truhe said. "She wants Darvon. I've given her some before. These people are a lot smaller than we are. They're not used to medicine. They get high on it. I'm not giving her any." He gave her a cigarette instead. She took the cigarette and made no more gestures toward her head.

In the next room a man lay on a plank bed giggling to himself. "What's the matter with him?" I asked.

"He's on something, probably opium," Truhe said.

"Do you have trouble with guys getting on the stuff with so much of it around here?" asked the wire-service reporter.

"Listen, there are too few of us here," said Truhe. "We depend too much on each other. I believe if I caught a guy on dope, I'd shoot him myself."

"Doc, do you remember that time we were pinned down in the cemetery and you looked around and said, 'Where is everybody?' and Dig said, 'This is it, This is CUPP 10'? We were the only ones left. Everybody else had been hit."

"Yeah," Truhe said, recalling the incident. "I said, 'Where is everybody?' and Dig said, 'This is it,' and I said, 'Is that right?'"

A Marine came in from another hootch. "Doc, can you give me something for my stomach?"

"What happened to that stuff they gave you at the Battalion Aid Station?"

"I took it but it didn't do any good. I can't eat these damn C rats."

"That's all I got, the same stuff they gave you at the aid station."

"I got an ulcer, Doc. I know I do. I can't eat these C rats. They just tear my stomach up. That doctor was pissed off at me because I had a cigarette before they x-rayed me and he told me not to. He couldn't find anything, but he was pissed off at me."

"Well, don't hang around in here. The VC see us bunched up in one hootch, and they'll put an RPG through it."

The sick Marine went back to his hootch, hunched against his gnawing guts. Doc Truhe had little sympathy for any hurt that didn't bleed, and it was easy to understand why. Every man in the team had ugly sores on his hands and feet. "Jungle rot," they called it. "Contact dermatitis," Truhe called it. Every one of them had frequent stomach cramps and diarrhea from a steady diet of C rations and malaria pills. They got high fever from the bad water, leeches from the rice paddies, and immersion foot from wet boots and socks. In addition, almost every peasant in the ville had some complaint.

In the next hootch, someone hacked and coughed. "TB," Truhe said. "In these villes the incidence of tuberculosis is about one out of twelve. It's a wonder we don't get it, living with them. We have to take tests for TB before we can go back to the world."

I watched as the Marines played with the children in the hootch, making them laugh. "What do you think of Calley?" asked a young, thin-haired Marine. He had the kind of face saints are pictured as having. Not effeminate but thin and angelic.

Calley had not been brought to trial, and all one heard in Vietnam were rumors and speculation. Not for one moment did I believe that Calley, or any other rational human being, could push the woman and children in the hootch into a ditch and deliberately shoot them. I didn't believe it because I couldn't credit another human being with doing something that I did not believe myself capable of doing in extremity or under duress. "I don't believe it," I said. "There is more to the story. There is some explanation."

"I think they ought to let him go," said the saintly faced Marine, who had spent almost a year defending the same kind of people Calley was supposed to have wasted.

"But what if he did it?"

"Oh, he did it all right. But why should he be the one punished?"

"You think he's a scapegoat for his superiors?"

"I think he's a scapegoat for the conscientious objectors."

I had heard everyone from President Kennedy to Ho Chi Minh blamed for My Lai, but I had never heard anyone blame the C.O.'s. "How do you mean?"

"I think they're like those people in New York who watched that woman being murdered. They don't want to get involved. They're moral cowards. They're afraid to have to decide whether or not to shoot into a ville because their buddies are being killed. They're afraid to have to shoot at some kid that's throwing frags at them. If their consciences are so great, why aren't they over here making those decisions instead of someone like Calley? They might save some lives besides their own. If everybody who has a conscience runs and hides, who do you have making moral decisions?"

"They're opposed to killing for any reason," I pointed out.

"They killed. That's what I think. They killed at My Lai. They're like referees. They want to stand on the sidelines and blow a whistle and say who's offside. I don't think that's conscientious. Hell, anybody can be conscientious when there's nothing at stake."

He picked up his rifle and went outside where the ambush was being organized. I followed him, and we walked along the footpaths, still muddy but not slick as before, and set up an ambush along a treeline that grew into the outskirts of the ville.

For a long time we sat on the wet ground, plagued by mosquitoes, watching the darkness as a fine mist fell. A few mortar shells fell far behind us, and an occasional flare changed the landscape from black to a garish green. I was almost asleep when the patrol leader came along passing the word that it was time to go.

We walked back to the night position, and then with the other Marines, we moved again, walking completely through the ville until we reached the river side of the hamlet. We were above the Ba Ren bridge. Across the river was an RF compound, and beyond the bridge and the Golf 2 C.P. was the ROK area of operation. The ROKs were receiving mortar fire.

"One night Charlie came along the river between us and the RFs with a loudspeaker," Truhe said. "He was telling the people what would happen to them if they didn't get out of this ville. It don't mean nothing though. We never did get him."

We watched the river for a while and then went inside the L-shaped hootch and spread our ponchos and liners on the ground. The papasan and his family lay on a plank bed which was curtained off with mosquito netting. I was beginning to understand the rationale for plank beds, which usually were nothing but sheets of plywood. Sometimes they had legs; sometimes they were placed on the floor. Either way they kept one off the wet earth, and they were cooler than lying on cotton mattresses.

The only light in the hootch was a candle burning in a C-ration can inside the curtains. Before the papasan blew out the light, a little girl raised her sleepy head and looked at us.

I lay down on the wet earth and tried to sleep. An occasional mortar landed across the river, jarring the ground. I wondered, as I had before, how the papasan and his family could sleep in the flimsy hootch when, for all they knew, the next mortar might land in the ville, or when even now VC sappers might be crawling through the ville with satchel charges. The peasants had so pitifully little, and what they possessed they held in fear. And it had gone on for so long. The French, the Japanese, the Viet Minh, the Viet Cong, the Americans. What did they dream of, these people? What did they hope for their children?

It was easy to understand the involvement the Marines felt with the people. A little girl had raised her head and looked at us before going back to sleep, assured that we were there for her protection. I hoped she slept better for our presence, although I knew, as the Marines knew, how fragile that protection was.

I went to sleep wondering how I would forget that child, trying to imagine how I could save her from the tragedy that engulfed her country. When I woke up it was still dark in the hootch, but I could see Kroft leaning against one of the bamboo poles that supported the roof. "What's the matter?" I asked, fearing he was sick.

"I find it more comfortable to stand than to lie down," he said.

I went back to sleep and woke again with the steel helmet I wore for a pillow digging into my neck. I joined Kroft, and we stood waiting for dawn to come. Once we went outside, but a light rain was falling, and we were afraid to move around for fear of being shot by the Marines or PFs on watch. When we went back inside, the children had a fire going in one corner of the hootch and were slowly feeding it wood shavings and straw to cook their rice. They hovered before the fire, shivering in the early morning damp.

Corporal Baldwin came over and gave the children some heat tabs on which to boil their rice. Lighting additional tabs, he prepared us some coffee and we drank it, sharing a canteen cup, and watched the children eat their rice, their eyes and mouths big in the light of the fire.

At first light we walked back through the ville to the C.P. Everyone there was talking about Corporal Roseberry's night operation, which had netted seventeen dead Viet Cong. They had listened to Roseberry's radio reports. Kroft and I said nothing. We were the outsiders, knowing nothing of what had happened. There had been a story and we had missed it. Yet, neither of us was certain it would have happened if we had been there. The patrol would have been larger; the route taken would have been safer. Who knows what would have happened?

The Regional Forces were punctual and orderly. Although the RFs were poorly trained, even by ARVN standards, this company appeared disciplined. The Marines attributed it to their very professional commander, Capt. Nguyen Le. Once, when an RF in a frivolous mood shot at a villager's chicken, the captain made the entire company get on their knees while he personally paid for the chicken. The RF had missed the chicken, but the captain paid for it anyway, and he made his men stay on their knees until they had learned their lesson.

During the recent typhoon the CUPP Marines had evacuated the villagers and then moved to the high ground at Baldy. The RFs had stayed and conducted at least one patrol each day while the VC were vulnerable. "I have been a soldier since fifteen," Captain Le said. "I will fight for my country as long as I live."

Most American military personnel believed that the Vietnamese fought well when they had good leadership, as was attested by the ability of the Viet Cong and NVA main forces and the best ARVN units. So why was a superb leader like Le only a captain? Politics, the Marines said. Le had a fighting spirit and a love for his country. To be a general he needed money or political power.

Lieutenant Smith organized the RFs and correspondents in four files, one file for each helicopter, and lined us up on the steel-girded Ba Ren bridge. Beside us was an older bridge of concrete. Two sections of the concrete bridge had been dropped into the river by the VC.

The helicopters were to land on the bridge and pick up the RFs as soon as it was light enough. However, the light was slow to come. Low, ragged clouds covered the sky and rain fell intermittently. After a while we could hear a lone helicopter as it flew over the bridge and continued on to Baldy. The helicopter reported that it could not see the bridge, the river, or the highway. At times the ceiling appeared to lift, and then a few minutes later heavy rain would fall. The neat files of RFs became ragged as the drenched men sat down and then bunched into groups.

"Charlie is either going to be gone, or he is going to be waiting for us," said a black Marine who was the platoon right guide. "They know we're coming by now."

Some of the RFs, becoming bored, shot at cans and other debris in the river. This caused excitement in the school behind the C.P. For a moment the chilren's faces jammed the windows of the cinder-block school, and then the teachers had them back in their places again.

The Marines grumbled over the unnecessary firing. "Save your ammunition; you're going to need it," some of them warned. Before long, some of the Marines were also shooting at targets in the river as contests developed between the Marines and between the Marines and RFs. Some of the correspondents tried their hand.

A couple of RFs went down to the river and tossed in grenades, picking up the stunned finger-long fish to boil for lunch.

Lieutenant Smith announced that the operation would be delayed until the weather cleared enough for the helicopters to get in. The RFs went back to their bunkers, the Marines went into the C.P., and the correspondents moved into the honcho's masonry house behind the C.P. The honcho and his wife retired into a curtained area of the one-room hootch, but their young son waited beside the door to tackle any Marine who came in. For a successful tackle he was thrown in the air, carried about, boxed with, and given C-ration candy.

The morning passed slowly as we waited for the helicopters. Some of the correspondents played cards; others smoked or read. The Marines talked about who was "shortest." Everyone kept track of the number of days of Vietnam service they had left. Baldwin referred to me as "an old hand."

I laughed because some of the correspondents had been in Vietnam for years. "What's an old hand?" I asked. "That's someone who shows pictures of his family to everyone he meets and invites everyone to come see him when they get home," Baldwin said.

Since nothing was going on, I changed my socks.

While I was in Da Nang, Mr. Tu, a Vietnamese correspondent, had taken me to the sprawling black market, which occupied several blocks. It was covered from the rain with tarpaulin and scraps of wood, all of it a foot lower than my head. Underfoot, to keep the goods and buyers out of the mud, were duckboards, broken crates, and wooden pallets. Foot-long rats and finger-length roaches scurried over and under the goods, chased by clouds of children.

Mr. Tu said, "Put your money in your hand and your hand in your pocket. I will guard your watch."

It was possible to buy Japanese watches, tape players, cameras, and televisions; American refrigerators and air conditioners; Vietnamese, Korean, Chinese, Russian, and American military uniforms, equipment, and rations; dried fish, imported wines, and exotic perfumes and firearms. The prices were better than military supply or PX, especially for large-size clothing, as they were too big for the Vietnamese.

I passed up the machine guns and flight suits and instead bought an extra set of Marine camouflage utilities, a canteen, and a pullover sweater that the Marines called a sleeping shirt. I intended to wear the sweater on cold nights. I also bought extra socks and tried to change them several times a day. I had tried to dry the socks by keeping them inside my jacket, but the air was so humid and I sweated so, it was useless.

While putting on fresh but not entirely dry socks, I noticed some dead-white places on my feet and discovered that the skin crumbled, like soft gum eraser. I was entertaining myself crumbling and brushing away the skin, when Baldwin said, "Better don't do that. That's like biting your lip when it's numb with Novocain."

We were getting bored and restless and began complaining to Smith about deadlines. The television crew in particular needed a story. The print reporters could file a story on Corporal Roseberry's operation, but the television team had nothing on film.

Lieutenant Smith clearly missed the simplicity of life as an enlisted man when he did his job the way it was supposed to be done. He despised the red tape and the public relations required to run a platoon when the cameras were present. Smith had not volunteered to be a diplomat.

Smith decided, if the helicopters couldn't get in, he would hike down to the island, ford the river, and assault. He asked how many reporters wanted to go. Most were willing to make the march, but the television team was undecided. They would have to carry the heavy cameras and battery packs, take a chance on losing the equipment in the river if a man fell or was shot, and unless the rain let up so there was enough light for filming, it would all be for nothing. After much discussion they decided to go. They needed a story, and this was the only one they had.

To walk to the island we had to cross through the Korean AOP (area of operation), and Lieutenant Smith had to get a clearance to be sure we did not cross one of their minefields or were mistaken for the enemy and fired upon. There was a delay as the clearance went up the chain of command.

Although the sky did not clear, the clouds lifted, and Lieutenant Smith was told the helicopters were coming. We lined up on the bridge and waited again. By noon nothing had happened with either the Koreans or the choppers. Smith called Captain Tilley and asked for permission to cancel the operation. There was another delay as the request went up the chain of command. Artillery and the support and medevac helicopters that had been standing by had to be notified that the operation was off. The RFs picked up their gear and marched back to their compound.

We, the correspondents, turned our disappointment on Smith. We had come for a story and he had not delivered. We had deadlines, quotas, obligations to fulfill and we had zilch, unless we wanted to do another story on military futility, fumbling, and red tape.

Smith said something to the effect that there were three platoons and each of them had a platoon-size operation two or three times a week. There were ten CUPP teams, and each had two patrols and an Alley Cat every day. We could go find our own stories.

Lieutenant Smith went into the C.P. We waited for another story or for a ride back to the cold beer, cheap drinks, and hot showers at the Da Nang Press Center.

Lieutenant McCay, who was to have gone on the island assault as artillery liaison, came over. "I'm going on an operation with Golf 1 [First Platoon] tomorrow," he said. "It's going to be a small one, but they think it's going to be interesting. You want to come?"

"Sure," I said, and we caught a jeep to Baldy to wait for transportation to Golf 1. Corporal Baldwin went along as my escort. A formation of PFs and Marines was standing before the company bunker. They had just completed the two-day school, and the PFs were being rewarded with extra gear before being sent back to their villes with their Marine counterparts.

Corporal Roseberry's patrol, having been out all night, had been sleeping on extra cots in one of the hootches. Kroft had gone to interview them, so Baldwin and I went to hear their story. They were sitting or lying on the cots and looked tired and half asleep. Roseberry, looking even thinner than before, went over the operation.

After dark the small patrol had made its first checkpoint without incident. The checkpoints were prearranged so that artillery could be provided in a hurry. The Marines moved from checkpoint to checkpoint after first scanning the area with a starlight scope.

"We saw two VC in a hole waiting for us," Roseberry said. "So we moved up on this hill and took up positions. From there we spotted seven more through the green eye. They were just sitting there waiting for us. We held our position, and after a while they began to group as though they were going to assault the hill, so we called for Blackhammer."

Blackhammer was a black-painted helicopter that flew at treetop level with infrared and other night-surveillance equipment and a high-power searchlight. Blackhammer was accompanied by three Huey gunships. When Blackhammer signaled the presence of humans, the searchlight was turned on them, and if they were carrying packs and rifles, the door gunners in the Hueys opened fire. Friendly units, such as Roseberry's team, carried strobe lights to identify their position.

"Before the helicopter got there, two VC tried to sneak up the hill and frag us," Roseberry said. "We didn't spot them until one of them raised up to throw a grenade, and then we shot both of them. Someone threw a grenade at them to make sure they were dead. The helicopter showed up while the VC were assembled to assault us, and they did a J.O.B. on them. We just sat and watched. It was like the Fourth of July."

After the helicopter attack the patrol swept down the hill through the VC position. One of the two VC who had crawled up the hill was still alive. "I heard him moan, so I shot him again," the machine gunner said. "You couldn't see, it was so dark, and he could have had a grenade or rifle in his hand. I know he was dead after I shot him though."

"How do you know he was dead?" asked Kroft, and the machine gunner smiled.

"He opened up on him with the M-60," said another Marine. "He set him on fire."

One man almost tripped a booby trap going down the hill. "There was a lot of low bushes, and I was going around them when I saw something. This VC must have been wounded and crawled under a bush to hide. When he saw me coming he looked up and I saw his eyes. I don't know what it was, but I saw something and I opened up, and this guy rolled out from under a bush. Lucky thing I saw him, because when I stopped to shoot I felt something brush against my leg. It was a trip wire. I backed up and went around the other way.

The Marines found seventeen bodies as they swept through the Viet Cong position. "We didn't touch them," Roseberry said, "because if there were any VC still alive, you can count on the bodies' being booby-trapped. They stick a frag under a body and pull the pin before they sky."

After the sweep, the patrol started back to Baldy and was ambushed by two more VC. "They jumped up and started shooting. We opened up and they skied. We found two blood trails that went into a bunker, so we fragged the bunker," Roseberry said.

"And after that you came back here?" Kroft asked.

Roseberry smiled sheepishly. "We got lost," the machine gunner said.

Roseberry ducked his head. "We got kind of turned around in all the excitement and had to call Baldy to fire a flare to guide us in. But we only had one casualty. One man got a fragment in his knee but he walked in OK. He didn't even go to the Battalion Aid Station. He just put a Band-Aid on it."

"Somebody was looking after us," said one young Marine. "God was pulling for us. He must have been."

"Everybody here likes being in a CUPP team," Roseberry said. "For one thing, you don't have to do a lot of humping like you do in line companies. Most of our operations take place right around here. Others feel that this is their chance to do something significant. This is a personal matter with us. You really get close to these people, and you can't help but get wrapped up in their problems. And it's a chance to show someone else what we've been taught. These PFs are damn good. If we were pulled out tomorrow, these guys would go on fighting."

Captain Tilley came by in a rage. "I just saw a gunner who does not deserve to be in the Marine Corps. Jesus. I was up in the command chopper, and we spotted this VC out in the open. He was carrying a rifle under his arm trying to hide it, but when we dropped down to look, he whipped it out and shot at us and took off for a treeline. He wasn't fifty meters from us, and the door gunner missed him with a machine gun, and he got away in the treeline. I was down on the floor trying to get my rifle between the gunner's legs. If I'd a got a shot, I would have dropped him.

"Too bad about that island operation," he apologized. "We get somebody every time we go out there. We've lost only one Marine though. I saw him get it. I was in the chopper, and we spotted this VC officer in the river behind the bank. Before we could get him this Marine looked over the bank, and the VC shot him in the head. Killed him instantly. The door gunner got that bastard though. He wasn't like the gunner we had today. The guy wasn't fifty meters away and he missed," he said, shaking his head in disbelief. "That man does not deserve to be in the Marine Corps."

First Platoon

Lieutenant McCay, Corporal Baldwin, and I were taken to the Golf 1 C.P., which was down the dirt road past the Golf 3 C.P. and CUPP 4's ville. The CUPP 4 Marines had no operation that day, and they were working at clearing the land and weeding the garden. The Golf 1 C.P., like that of Golf 3, was situated on a hill. This hill however was longer and not so steep, and the jeep climbed easily past the barbed-wire gate. The C.P. was of one level but was built in two parts around an enormous boulder that dominated the hill. There was also a bunker lower down the hill for RFs who helped defend the hill. Between the RF bunkers and the Marine bunker was a mortar pit. Lt. Charles Stafford, platoon commander, came out of the C.P. to greet us.

Lieutenant Stafford was the largest officer in the company, although he didn't look it. He didn't have the aggressive impatience of Lieutenant Smith, the handsome refinement of Lieutenant McDonnell, or the aura of command of Captain Tilley. He looked gangling, baby-faced, and country, and his voice carried the soft whine of his native Georgia. Although he looked young enough to be fresh out of boot camp, Lieutenant Stafford had served a tour in the Mediterranean. He had played war games with the French Foreign Legion—"They never did announce who won"—and had taken part in NATO military exercises. There was a likable, unspoiled boyish quality about him, and his experience and judgment belied his youthful look.

Lieutenant McCay noticed a few changes in the C.P. "We've filled boo coo sandbags," said Lieutenant Stafford. "But we're about finished."

A month earlier, the Golf 1 C.P. had been attacked and nearly overrun by the VC. "They hit us with a mortar attack, and the sappers came right in behind it. They got through the wire, hit the C.P. and set it on fire, and almost overran us. I think they would have, except that one of their RPGs hit some CS gas we had stored behind the C.P. and blew it all over everything. It's not really a gas; it's more like a powder and it just covered everything.

"I didn't know what had happened at first. I couldn't breathe, I couldn't move. It's not harmful, but everywhere it touches you it burns like fire. It gets in your eyes and you can't see, and if you rub them that just makes it worse. It gets in your nose and ears. Man, you think you're going to die. Your nose drains, your eyes water. It just immobilizes you. You can't even think. All you can do is stand there and wait for it to wear off. I think the VC panicked when the gas hit them. They just pulled out. We were lucky. We're pretty isolated up here. We can get a reaction force from Baldy, but it takes a while for them to get here, and they've got to come down that road. When they do, Charlie's going to have it mined, with an ambush set up."

Lieutenant Stafford pointed out one Marine who had stayed in the mortar pit firing the mortar until the VC threw a grenade in the pit. He jumped out of the pit, but the grenade destroyed the mortar. He jumped back in the pit and held off the VC with his rifle. "I recommended him for a medal," Stafford said, "but I won't recommend him for a promotion. He's no leader. He can fight but he can't carry responsibility."

During the attack, Lieutenant Stafford had been in a sandbagged fighting hole when he was called to the radio inside the burning C.P. While he was on the radio, a B40 rocket destroyed the position he had just left. "That was a lucky call I got," he said.

Lieutenant Stafford was going to check the three teams going on the operation the next day and he invited me along. We rode along the dirt road between rice paddies and uncleared fields. Beside the road was a piece of twisted metal, unidentifiable except for part of a steering wheel still attached to it. For several meters in every direction were scraps of metal no larger than a man's hand.

"That's the only mining incident we've had on this road in six months," Stafford said. "That was an ARVN six by." A "six by" was the Marine equivalent of the Army's "deuce and a half," or 2½-ton truck. "Luckily the driver was the only one in it. They had to pick him up with a shovel. I had just gone by there in a jeep. Evidently it was an antitank mine, and the jeep wasn't heavy enough to detonate it. It left quite a crater in the road. Must have been three or four hundred pounds of TNT."

It was hard to sit back in the jeep and relax after that, hard not to cringe at every mound or depression or object lying in the road, any of which might signify the presence of a mine.

As he conferred with the squad leaders and handed out the ammo resupply, Lieutenant Stafford also pointed out the accomplishments of his men. CUPP 1 had helped the villagers build a pagoda and school, which were newly finished and painted. CUPP 2 had captured a VC nurse who had given the battalion some valuable information. They had also captured a man who identified himself as an NVA soldier. "There's an NVA unit back in there. We may run into them tomorrow. Things have been quiet around CUPP 3 lately, but their turn will come."

I wanted to know if those things really mattered. In this kind of world, this kind of war, what good was a pagoda and a school and a few gardens? What difference did it make?

"Those are tangible results," Stafford said. "You can see a school or pagoda. And if the gardens improve the diet of these people, it's going to make a difference for the rest of their lives."

What about intangibles? I wanted to know. Were there any lasting effects?

"You guys criticize the military for not knowing anything about the history and culture of these people, and rightly so. We don't know much about them. But you guys are no better. You don't understand them any better than we do.

"Do you think we've been here a long time? They don't think so. How many clocks have you seen in the villes? How many calendars? They don't count minutes, they count generations. And we haven't been here long enough for them to count. They don't count our arrival as yesterday yet. They think the Americans got here today.

"Another thing. This is a pluralistic society. They don't draw distinctions like we do; if you're a Republican you can't be a Democrat. They don't think like that. These people worship their ancestors. And Buddha. And Confucius. Some of them worship spirits. And those who have heard about Jesus worship him too. And Mohammed. They don't think if you're a Buddhist you can't be a Hindu or can't worship Jesus at the same time. What do you think it sounds like when we say, 'You got to be for us or you're Viet Cong'? They think we're simple. They like the government, and they like us, and they like the Viet Cong, and they like Ho Chi Minh, those that have heard of him. They don't have any problems with that. We're the ones who have a problem with it.

"We're trying to cope with it, and I think the press should be educating people, helping them to understand what life is like here, instead of lists of bombs dropped, villages pacified, people killed. That doesn't mean anything."

I pointed out that the information MAC-V released was bombs dropped, villages pacified, people killed.

"I thought you guys were supposed to go out and get your own news. The story behind the story, and all that. People back home don't have any way of understanding what's going on here because they don't have any background to build on. Granted, we're not doing a good job of educating them, but is it our job? I'm sure MAC-V and the Pentagon would leap to the occasion, but I'm not sure the press would allow it."

I said that the media, and maybe the folks back home, would not place great credence on information that came only from MAC-V and the Pentagon.

"That's what I'm saying," Stafford said. "The government is lying. The military is lying. The press is lying. Everyone is lying. Either that, or everyone is giving facts and figures. And if you don't have any way of adding up the facts and figures, they lie. If you don't have a story to put them in, or a philosophy to wrap around them, well, facts and figures are just lies."

In one village, Lieutenant Stafford pointed out a young boy. "The VC came into the ville one night and told that boy to get his things, that he was going with him. That's the age they like to recruit them—thirteen or fourteen. They went off to round up some more boys, and when they came back the kid threw two frags at them. Since then he hasn't been able to sleep at home because they're looking for him. He stays with the Marines."

I think Lieutenant Stafford was inviting me to write a story about the boy. It would be a difficult interview because I didn't speak Vietnamese, and hard to write because I would have to explain how the VC and the Marines both lived in a tiny ville of less than a hundred families. And if I wrote it, who in the United States would read such a story?

In another ville, Stafford said, "There's a crazy man that lives in that ville. The Vietnamese say he's been crazy his whole life, but no reporter thinks so. Every time someone comes out here to do a story, he runs up to them and froths at the mouth and rolls on the ground, and they report he was driven crazy by the bombing. They don't bomb these villes. We live here."

That may have been another invitation to a story. If so, Stafford's understanding of what the media was about and what the American public wanted to know was, at best, limited.

When we got back to the C.P., Lieutenant Stafford outlined the operation. "We're going into Happy Valley tomorrow. We haven't been in there in a long time, and we think the VC or maybe the NVA is in there. CUPP 1 and 3 are going to move out as soon as they can see. One will go up each side of the valley and set up blocking positions. Then we'll walk right up the middle with CUPP 2. If Charlie stays we'll get him, and if he runs, CUPP 1 and 3 will be waiting for him."

It was a quiet night. Low-lying clouds blotted out the stars and sometimes even flares that popped unseen high in the air and slowly drifted down out of the clouds like enormous, slow-falling stars. The CUPP team, lying in ambush outside the ville, reported no movement. A thin yellow cat skulked around the mortar pit, the first cat I had seen in Vietnam. "We've adopted that cat," Stafford said. "It's not very tame. You don't see many cats here. I don't know whether the Vietnamese eat them or the rats do. Cats are no match for the rats around here."

Stafford gave us some Long Rats—chile con carne—and some C4 to boil water. I was leery of lighting the C4, an explosive, but it was safe to burn and boiled water much faster than heat tabs. Stafford also offered Tabasco sauce. Almost every grunt had his own bottle of hot sauce. It added flavor to the bland rations, and there was a perverse pleasure in eating hot, spicy food in a hot climate. One more thing to sweat about.

The food was good. While eating, I realized it was the first time I had eaten all day. I had one meal yesterday, one today. The Marines seemed to eat whenever they thought of it. I had noticed that when there was a lull in the fighting most of the men pulled out cigarettes and favorite snacks they had saved from their rations. Some of them ate entire meals, three or four meals within a few hours. I think they were rewarding themselves with some brief pleasure, celebrating the fact they were still alive.

A CUPP leader called to report that one of his men had a high fever and that the corpsman was unable to get it down. "Has he been taking his malaria pills?" Stafford asked. "I'm not calling a medevac after dark. Helicopters draw too much fire, and Charlie will start dropping mortars on the ville. Tell the corpsman to keep him cool until after road sweep, and I'll send a jeep for him in the morning."

Two Marines gave up their cots so that Baldwin and I would have a place to sleep. After sleeping on the ground, I found the cot a luxury. In the villes I slept with my boots on, leaving them unlaced for circulation, and after putting on dry socks if I had them. But Baldwin and I pulled off our wet, heavy boots, stripped off the damp socks, stretched out, and wiggled our toes in the air. "I feel like a candy ass," Baldwin said.

It was a peaceful night—one of those nights you wish would last forever. Instead, it ended well before dawn.

We got our things together by flashlight and stumbled over the gear-littered floor and around the boulder to the other side of the C.P. where Lieutenant Stafford was cooking breakfast. In addition to the cat, First Platoon was also unique in the fact that they always had a hot breakfast at the C.P., cooked on a gas-operated camp stove. The men took turns cooking, and today it was Stafford's turn. Lieutenant Stafford was scrambling eggs by candlelight and scooping them out in the paper plates held by his men. In addition to the eggs there were thick slices of bread and hot coffee. We ate quickly because CUPP 1 and 3 were getting ready to move.

Outside it was just light enough to distinguish large masses. Lieutenants McCay and Stafford and Baldwin and I got in the jeep for the ride to CUPP 2. "The toughest part is going to be driving down the road before it's been swept for mines, but it's better than walking," Stafford said, easing the jeep through the barbed-wire gate and then driving slowly enough to detect objects in the road or signs of freshly disturbed earth.

We rode without speaking, absorbed in a study of the road. I half squatted in the back of the jeep, supporting my weight on the balls of my feet in the insane hope that if we detonated a mine I could jump unharmed into the air. After a few minutes the jeep ground to a stop. We had reached the RF compound. The RFs, living in earth bunkers just off the road, guarded a wooden bridge and kept the road closed until the mine sweep from Baldy had cleared it.

Leaving the jeep, we walked through the wire gate, over the bridge, and through the RF compound. At the gate on the opposite side of the compound, a crowd of Vietnamese peasants had gathered. They were mostly women, supporting "dummy sticks" across their frail shoulders. Hanging balanced on either end of the sticks were baskets of vegetables, firewood, and pigs, bound for the markets down the road. They were waiting for the mine sweep to clear the road, after which the RFs would open the gates and check the baskets for weapons, ammo, or mines. The peasants watched us pass without curiosity or interest.

We walked down the road, stepping in the tracks the Vietnamese had left, passing again the remains of the ruined ARVN truck. We could hear firing. "Who's that?" Stafford asked.

"That's the CUPP 1 machine gunner," a Marine said. "I'd recognize that rhythm anywhere."

After a few more meters we left the road, with a sigh of relief, and crossed a weedy, uncleared field to the ville where CUPP 2 was waiting. "CUPP 1 has heavy contact and has called for a medevac," they called as soon as we were close enough to hear. Stafford hurried to the radio for a situation report. "OK, get your PFs ready," he told the CUPP 2 leader. "We're going to react."

The men were ready, and without another word we followed a footpath through the ville, across some rice paddies, through a treeline, and plunged into a cane field so high and thick that we could see nothing except the man ahead and the narrow path at our feet. As we broke out of the cane field, we could hear firing ahead of us.

The sky was gray and overcast, and in the humidity sweat popped out on my forehead and began to run into my eyes and soak through the camouflage suit. Stafford called a brief halt. CUPP 3, on our right, had also run into contact, and Stafford wanted to know their situation before we moved any farther. CUPP 3 had taken fire from a small hill. There were no casualties. CUPP 3 was carrying a 60mm mortar with them, and they plastered the top of the hill, chasing off the VC. Stafford decided to continue to the relief of CUPP 1.

We passed through more rice fields and into a small ville in a treeline. Not a single human was in sight, but as we followed a footpath through the ville, I spotted green uniforms on the opposite side of the ville. I had a few anxious moments before Baldwin identified them as PFs who had gotten ahead of the column. The Marines quickly checked the empty hootches and then moved on, but we were not walking so fast now. The firing had stopped and everything was deadly still. Charlies had di-died. The column moved slowly as the Marines checked side trails and treelines before moving on.

As we came around the side of a little hill, two Cobra gunships passed overhead. CUPP 1 had chased their attackers into a thicket, and we stopped until the Cobras had pounded them with rockets and miniguns. After the gunships' last run, we swept through the thicket.

It was called a sweep, but it was nothing like the picture the word brought to mind — a line walking abreast through the jungle and looking under every bush. Because of the thickness of the brush we could move only along trails or footpaths or across clearings through the thicket. Baldwin pointed out a line of chopped turf about a foot wide. It was the path of a minigun that put one bullet per square inch in a foot-wide trail through the target area.

The rockets had left gashes in the earth, but they weren't craters the way I had imagined. The only crater I saw was an old one after we had pushed through the thicket. "Probably a 105," Baldwin said. It was the first crater I had seen. The rains and farmers quickly obliterated any signs of battle.

Again there was firing to our right, and we pushed through another thicket and came out at a river bank. As the firing continued, we slid down the high steep bank and into the swift current of the waist-deep river. The water was shockingly cold. A PF tapped me on the shoulder and handed me a canteen that had been torn loose by my slide down the bank.

On the other side of the river was a level area of some thirty meters and then another high bank. We splashed out of the river and huddled under that bank and worked to our left until the bank curved back to the river's edge. Suddenly, directly in front of me, at the point where the bank met the river, a tree exploded. For a moment I didn't know what had happened and could only stare at the smoke and dirt rising where the tree leaned brokenly across the river.

I turned around at some commotion behind me. The PF honcho had struck one of his men. "That's right, knock the shit out of him," Stafford said, and the honcho hit him again. One of the PFs had accidentally triggered a LAW, which had hit the tree in front of us. No one had been injured, but there was muttering and cursing as the Marines climbed over the bank and headed in the direction of the firing.

Abruptly the shooting stopped. We came to a stream at the end of a broad rice field and set up a blocking position and waited. Nothing happened. A PF, spotting movement in a field some distance away, opened fire with his M-16 without hitting anything. "What's he shooting at?" several Marines asked. One of them put binoculars on the field and yelled, "Knock it off, that's a babysan." The shooting stopped. "That's a little kid with a water bull," he said.

After a few minutes we were humping again, this time along a path beside a treeline. The trail was almost five feet wide and was about three feet higher than the water in the rice paddy. The treeline was so thick we couldn't see into it. The trail made a curve, and as we followed it a broad valley of rice fields expanded in front of us. A rusting armored personnel carrier with one track missing lay on its side in the rice field—the victim of a mine in some earlier forgotten battle. Stafford turned and looked at me. "Welcome to Happy Valley," he said.

As we made our way around the broad curve of the trail, I could see that in the middle of the valley was an island of high ground, overgrown with trees. At the near end of the island a masonry pagoda with a red tile roof protruded from the vegetation. A sound came across the rice paddy like someone sharply knocking sticks together and the Marines dropped. I fell too as firing erupted around me.

I raised the rifle, pushed the helmet out of my eyes, aimed at the island—there was no target to shoot at—and fired. I wasn't trying to be a hero or to play Marine. It wasn't a conscious decision at all. I suspect my motive was fear. We were a small unit under fire, and I could not afford the luxury of being a spectator.

I confess to an urge to jump up and charge across 150 meters of sucking mud, madly firing the rifle. Where do such impulses come from? I suspect the movies. The Marines had had such irrational impulses trained out of them. I successfully resisted mine.

Above the firing I could hear the word being passed, "Doc up." I passed it too, although a hunched-over corpsman was already running past me to fall a few feet away.

Every man around me was firing, and the earth about the pagoda jumped and splattered under the hail of bullets. I put down the rifle, picked up the camera, and took a few pictures of the pagoda, although I knew very well how the snapshots would look—a wide expanse of rice paddy with the tiny red dot of the pagoda roof barely visible in the island greenery. I also imagined what I would say about the photograph: "We were taking fire from that pagoda, and it was a lot closer than it looks in the picture."

I turned and took a couple of pictures of the Marines and PFs lying on the trail and firing. I also knew how those photographs would look, more like Marines on a rifle range than Marines in combat. "No, really, they're shooting at somebody," I'd have to explain.

I raised up to get a picture of the corpsman lying on his side with his back to the enemy. It was hard to imagine a man exposing himself like that. The trail we were on was like a shelf above the rice field, scarcely wide enough for a man to lie across it at an angle. The only protection was to lie low. From the island probably all the VC could see was a few helmeted heads and the wide back of one corpsman. Beside the corpsman, lying on his face, was Lieutenant Stafford.

The firing played out and then stopped. Only two or three minutes had passed since the firing broke out. No one moved, but the word passed down the line—Lieutenant Stafford had been hit in the hand. No one knew how serious it was. In the movies, a hand wound was something a cowboy wrapped his bandanna around, but in the rice paddies a bullet sometimes tore off a hand or arm.

We lay waiting. One Marine kept looking nervously behind him into the treeline. He was afraid of the VC getting in behind him. Taking two other Marines, he got up and moved back along the trail until he found an opening in the treeline. A few minutes later another Marine looked up. "I hear something behind us," he said. I told him some Marines were back there. He also went for a look. I followed him back to the opening through the treeline and down the footpath. Hidden in the trees behind us was a small ville. The Marines checked the hootches. I went back and lay down on the trail. It seemed safer.

Lieutenant McCay sent five Marines farther up the trail we were on as security for the medevac helicopter that was now in sight. Baldwin and I went with them. McCay popped a red smoke in the paddy beside Lieutenant Stafford. As the helicopter came in for a landing, the Marines began firing again to keep the VC down.

The helicopter, a large Sea Knight, set down slowly in the rice paddy, landing on the two rear wheels and keeping the front wheels in the air so that it did not sink into the mud. The corpsman supported Lieutenant Stafford against the blast of the rotors as he crossed the paddy and stepped into the chopper. As the helicopter lifted off, I could see the gunner open up on the island with the .50-caliber machine gun. I couldn't tell whether or not the chopper was being fired on.

As the medevac pulled out of sight, two Cobras came in for a run on the island. The pagoda disappeared in the smoke and dust thrown up by the rockets. There was something satisfying about watching the helicopters work. I joined the Marines in having a warm regard for them. They were looking after me.

Baldwin and I had been sitting up rather carelessly watching the helicopters, and suddenly the water in front of us erupted, something hit the ground beside us, and something slammed into my foot. We hit the ground in panic. "What was that?" Baldwin asked. I raised my head slowly to look at my foot. It felt numb but was not marked in any way. With one hand I reached back and touched my foot to reassure myself. Baldwin reached into the grass and pulled out something shiny. Shell casings from the helicopter's machine guns had fallen harmlessly around us, and one of them had hit my foot.

In the absence of Lieutenant Stafford, Lieutenant McCay took charge. "I'm going to have to rely on the squad leaders," he said to the radio operator. "They know the area better than I do."

CUPP 3 was in sight off to our right. They were crossing a treeline along a stream that ran at a right angle to our position, and incredibly they were plunging into the open rice paddy and humping toward the island from which we were taking fire. "Tell CUPP 3 to get in the trecline and spread out," Lieutenant Mc-Cay told the radio operator, who relayed the message. The Marines spread out along the treeline and began advancing on the island.

The radio operator passed on more orders, but still CUPP 3 continued to advance. Lieutenant McCay took the radio and asked for the CUPP 3 Actual—the squad leader. "Tell those men to execute a 180 and get out of the rice paddy and set up a base of fire in the treeline," McCay said. With what seemed to be reluctance, CUPP 3 turned and walked back into the trees.

When McCay was certain they had set up a blocking position, he led CUPP 2 through the opening in the treeline and into the ville behind. In the center of the ville, on a slight mound, sat about a dozen women and children. There was not a male present over eight years of age.

One of the Marines called the corpsman over to look at a wound in the back of one of the women. The wound was an old one and was covered by a dirty dressing. "VC bandage," the corpsman said. He threw it away, applied a disinfectant to the wound, and rebandaged it. While he was doing this, the PF honcho asked one of the women how many VC there were. She said there were twenty-four.

Fire erupted again from the island and fell in the ville. The peasants scattered, running to their bunkers. The Marines and PFs ducked behind trees. A black machine gunner had his M-60 in action before he hit the ground.

"That's why I didn't want those guys out in the open paddy," McCay said, almost apologetically.

There wasn't much return fire from the Marines this time, just the M-60 and a few rifles. The rest of us took cover. The Marines turned out, so that someone was facing in every direction. The Marines expected to be hit from the flanks. I gripped the M-16, not believing I could hit anything with it, but thinking I might have to use it to keep the enemy at bay. Old lessons came to mind—to aim low because a bullet aimed too high was a miss, but a bullet too low might ricochet into the enemy position or kick up enough dirt to keep the enemy's head down. Although it hadn't registered at the time, I remembered how mild mannered the M-16 was. My experience with military weapons had been with the M-1 and the B.A.R., weapons that left bruises on one's shoulders.

The Cobras were back, and under their protection we were going to run about 150 meters across a paddy dike and onto the island. The machine gun would provide a base of fire, and the Marines would keep a wide interval. They were to keep moving if a man went down. The wounded would be taken care of once a secure force was on the island. As the first few men on the paddy dike did not draw fire. I was inserted into the file and told to run. I ran, head down, trying only to avoid falling into the paddy, knowing that Baldwin was behind me and would stay with me if I was hit. The man in front of me went down, sprawling in the mud. I thought he had been hit and slowed, but he jumped up, cursing and splashing out of the paddy and onto the dike.

Once we had reached the island, we ducked into cover. As soon as the last man had reached the safety of the trees, the Cobras left. We formed up for a sweep of the island.

The island was covered with groves of trees. In the clearings grass grew waist to shoulder high. The Marines walked slowly through the grass, spreading out over the trails. After a few meters down one of the trails, we came to five or six hootches. In an open area in front of the hootches about a dozen women and children were squatting and smiling as though to have their picture taken.

Although I had seen it before, I was always astonished to see women and children sitting in the middle of the ville awaiting our arrival. Where had they come from? Where had they been during the shooting? Why were they smiling? In friendly villes, the people paid no more attention to the Marines than to the PFs. In neutral villes visited by both the Marines and the VC, the villagers sat impassively in front of their hootches so as to constitute no threat and arouse no suspicion. These people were squatting in rows as though for inspection, smiling like shopkeepers. There were no males over eight years of age.

The Marines looked into the hootches. One Marine found an ammo can with the lid closed on it. Fearing it was booby-trapped, he called one of the small boys over. The mother held to the boy's hand. The Marine got the boy, led him to the can, and asked him to open it. The Marines believed the peasants knew what was mined and that they would not go into an area that was mined or touch anything that was booby-trapped. The ammo can was empty, but the act made the Marine a war criminal. It was a violation of the Geneva Convention to use civilians to discover mines and booby traps, and the rule had always made sense to me. However, had I been that Marine in that ville, I would have done the same as he.

The Marines poked through the piles of rubbish around the ville looking for rice or arms caches. One PF found a new pot hidden in a pile of rubbish and tied it to his belt. Another PF confiscated a mess of fish. A Marine came out of a hootch with something shiny that he showed to Lieutenant McCay and then to me. It was a French Indochina coin dated 1954. The coins were widely believed to be used to identify VC couriers. The woman smiled at us.

The PFs took one of the small boys and pulled off his shirt. While one of them held his arms, another held a knife at his stomach and questioned him. Where was his father? Where were the men of the village? Where were the VC? The boy said nothing, possibly because he didn't know, possibly because he had been threatened with worse things if he told, probably because his father was a Viet Cong.

A Marine told the PF with the knife that the boy was not to be harmed. The PF shrugged. Someone from this ville had shot at him. He asked more questions. The boy cried. The women smiled. The PFs released the boy, who was now a hero in the ville, and we walked through the ville and along the footpaths through the woods and grass. The Marines spotted blood trails.

We followed the paths until they led us to the pagoda. Along one side of the pagoda was a deep trench with fresh footprints. It had been from that trench that the VC had fired at us. We sat down around the pagoda to rest. The sun had dried up the clouds, and it was hot and sticky. CUPP 3 was sitting in the treeline to our front across the rice paddy.

We walked around the pagoda, through some trees, across a ditch, and to the edge of the island where a paddy dike ran from the island to CUPP 3's treeline. As the first man started across the paddy dike, he was fired on. He dropped into the mud behind the dike. Lieutenant McCay, directly in front of me, was lying in mud and water. I squatted down in the paddy and hugged the bank of the island, which was three or four feet above the water. I tried to cock the M-16 but it jammed. I swore at the weapon, imagining how a man might regard the rifle in a stress situation.

"Take out the magazine," said Baldwin, who squatted beside me. I did and it worked.

The firing was coming from the ville where the corpsman had treated the woman's back. "They pulled out while we were there and then came back," McCay said.

I thought suddenly of the Marine who believed that men who were proud of their conscience should be in Vietnam. Here was the place for such a man. We were taking fire from a ville, and we knew there were women and children in that ville. We had seen them. And if those people were Viet Cong, then Charlie had little regard for his own people because the VC on the island had fired into the ville while we were in it.

The Marines could not get artillery or air support to fire into that ville, but to get off the island they had to cross the open paddy dike. They either had to lay down covering fire into the ville or cross the paddy under automatic-rifle fire and take almost certain casualties. I had never looked at the problem that way before, and as one of those who had to cross the paddy, I was no longer philosophical about it. I wanted lots of fire on the enemy position in the ville while I was exposed on the dike. I was firmly, if conveniently, convinced that the women and children were safely in their bunkers. McCay must have felt the same way. "Get ready to move out," he yelled.

CUPP 3, from its position in the treeline, laid down a base of fire as we ran single file across the dike. It was a long run on the narrow, muddy dike in a heavy flak jacket with the helmet bouncing on my head. I got off the dike, ducked behind a mound of dirt, and panted for breath. When I caught my breath and looked around, I saw that CUPP 3 was not in the treeline at all but behind the bank of a small stream. A few scattered trees grew along the bank. A wooden footbridge was built over the stream, and at our end of the bridge a mound of earth had been built as the approach to the bridge to keep it above the water of the rice field. That was the mound I was lying behind.

As the last few men ran across the paddy dike, we began to take fire from the island we had just left. The Marines returned the fire, and a few seconds later we were fired on from our right, so that we were under fire from three directions. As we were all bunched up around the bridge, McCay moved people around to better positions. McCay's face was red and his glasses steamy from the run across the paddy dike, but he was white around the mouth.

Baldwin and I waded back into the rice field and squatted in the mud behind the dike. I tucked the camera inside my flak jacket to keep it out of the water. In the water of the paddy I could see the vee of a snake that we had disturbed. "Bamboo viper," I said. I didn't know what kind of snake it was, but I knew bamboo vipers were poisonous. The stone-faced Baldwin ignored me. Two Marines who heard me stood up and walked out of the paddy.

The situation was not desperate but it was dangerous. Nevertheless, the Marines moved as casually as though it were a training exercise. Occasionally one would stand and, with only his head ducked, move to a better position. One Marine sat on the ground firing his M-16. The mortar crew from CUPP 3 set up the mortar on the high ground before the bridge and dropped the last of their shells on the near end of the island.

One Marine stood up, looked around, and yelled, "Hey, where are the PFs?" The PFs were gone. In the paddy behind us a water buffalo had been hit by a stray round, and while we had been taking fire from three sides, the PFs had crowded around the buffalo butchering it with bayonets. The Marines yelled at them to get under cover. The VC discovered them about the same time as the Marines, and bullets started hitting the ground around them. The PFs ran for cover with huge steaks streaming blood down their shoulders.

Beside me a Marine crawled out of the paddy with leeches stuck to his leg. The corpsman removed them with insecticide. Baldwin and I crawled out of the paddy also; the snake and leeches were too much. We went back to the mound behind the mortar crew.

"How old are you?" one of the men asked. I confessed my thirty-eight years. "I can't believe you old guys are out here playing war," he said.

Was that what we were doing? Playing war? In a way, yes, we all were. We were playing a deadly game so that folks back home would know what it was like. Were we doing as bad a job as Stafford said? Nothing I had read or seen back in the world had prepared me to understand a ville, or shooting into a ville, or using civilians to detect mines and booby traps. And nothing in my education and experience, nothing in philosophy, religion, or literature, had prepared my conscience to make the decisions these young men were forced to make.

Lieutentant McCay turned to me. "We can go back over there and look for them, but they'll just keep pulling back until they've got us surrounded," he said. "If Stafford or some infantry officer were here, it would be different, but I'm going to cancel the operation and get out of here. They'll try to ambush us on the way back."

The Cobras were back overhead, and while they made dummy runs to keep the VC down, we crossed the footbridge and started along a path on the other side. As we pulled back the PFs joined the column. They carried helmets full of fresh meat. More meat swung from sticks across their shoulders. The two Cobras circled low over us to break up any ambush.

We moved fast, as the trail was wide and solid. Along the trail at regular fifty-meter intervals were water-filled holes, just big enough for a man's body. They had been dug there for protection from bombs and artillery fire. The recent rains had filled them. The trail passed between a cane field and a rice field, and as I came around a turn, there on the trail in front of me was the projectile from a 175mm cannon.

It looked enormous lying there in the open, shockingly big and out of place. If it was a dud, wouldn't its nose be sticking in the ground? If it was a booby trap, wouldn't it be concealed in some way? I looked at the back of the man ahead. He was moving fast, trying to get away from it before I tripped it or before it was command-detonated by a VC hiding in the cane field.

The strategy was to keep a wide interval, offering only one man to an enemy who might be lying in concealment ready to detonate the shell. The enemy, however, would be able to choose that man. My hope was that I did not look like an officer.

I waited until the man ahead of me disappeared around another turn in the trail, and then I walked past, fast but under control, unable to look directly at it but watching for trip wires and stepping in the footprints of the man before me.

Soon we reached the river, and as we bunched up to cross the swift current, I turned to the impassive Baldwin. "Did you see that?" I was like a kid who had seen a ghost or dragon and would not believe his eyes until someone assured him that he wasn't dreaming or that his mind hadn't failed him.

"Yeah, it was a 175. They'll have to send an EOD [Explosive Ordnance Demolition] team out to blow it. The CUPPs don't have anything big enough to detonate it."

"What was it doing on the trail?"

"Someone put it there," Baldwin said. He shrugged.

I slipped off the bank and plunged into the cold swift current. It felt good.

The Cobras circled us all the way back to CUPP 2's ville. The Marines fell on the ground and began stripping off their wet boots and socks. "Babysan, wash," they told the children who were waiting to run errands or buy soft drinks. I pulled off my helmet and flak jacket and sat down to wait for the platoon jeep. I was surprised to discover that when I relaxed my muscles quivered.

"I bet right now Charlie is laughing at us," said one Marine, plainly disgusted with the outcome of the operation. "We took two casualties and we didn't get shit."

"He wasn't laughing when the Cobras came in," said another. "We got some. I saw the blood."

"The mortarman told me he dropped a round right on top of the VC firing at them from the hill. He knows he got one of them. He saw him bounce."

"Hitting him and finding him are two different things."

"What we ought to do next time is land a platoon by helicopter at the far end of the valley, and then we sweep through it and get every VC in there."

"How was Lieutenant Stafford?" I asked the corpsman.

"He was in a lot of pain but it didn't look bad. The bullet was still there. A hand's a funny thing. There's a lot of little bones in there, and a bullet will really mess them up. It'll probably be stiff the rest of his life, but I don't think he'll lose it."

"Every time we get an officer who knows what's going on, he gets shot," someone said.

Blackhammer

The jeep taking us back to Baldy struck and killed a dog in the ville CUPP 4 lived in, and the children came running out in the road to look. The dog had run into the road, and although the driver had swerved to miss the dog, the trailer ran over it. It occurred to me that I had never seen a Vietnamese dog chase a jeep or bicycle or anything else. Neither had the driver. "You don't see them playing either," he said. "Dogs over here are different. They know they're going to be eaten."

Captain Tilley was waiting back at the company office to hear more about the operation. The sun was shining, and he had his utility jacket open to soak up the rays. Above his navel was a ragged white scar to remind him of his first tour in Vietnam.

Tilley and Staff Sergeant Shivers were talking to a three-man scout-sniper team who were waiting for a ride out to the bush. Intelligence said that a courier would be coming down the trail bringing plans and messages. At dusk the team would set up overlooking the trail. They would lie quietly all night, shoot the man and take his papers, and leave his body on the trail to demoralize the VC. The snipers claimed the ability to hit a man half a mile away. "The sound echoes around the hills, and they have no way of knowing where the shot came from. They have no way of knowing whether or not they can be seen or who will be next. It works on them."

"You can tell when a sniper has been in the area," another said. "Charlie won't move in the daytime, and when he does he is real slow. He ducks from cover to cover. It slows them down."

The snipers were older than the CUPP Marines, and graver. They were pros, and they handled the sniper rifles with careful but familiar ease, the detachment of the specialist.

After the snipers left, Captain Tilley and Sergeant Shivers listened as McCay went over the operation. McCay was uncertain as to whether he had done the right thing in canceling the operation.

"Where was Lieutenant Stafford when he was hit?" asked Captain Tilley.

"He was between two radiomen," McCay said. "He was walking behind his radioman, and my radioman was walking ahead of me."

"Then they weren't just spraying the trail; they were aiming at him," Tilley said. "They picked him out."

"Do you think it was VC snipers in spider holes?" Shivers asked.

"It sounds like the NVA to me," Captain Tilley said. "I've seen that happen before. A few people will shoot at you and pull back and you get to chasing them, and the first thing you know they're all around you, and they've got you outnumbered, and they start closing in. Intelligence says there's an NVA unit in there."

"We're going to have to go back in company size and chase them out," McCay said.

"How did you like your air support?" Tilley asked. "The old man was looking after you wasn't he?"

"That was great," said McCay. "I figured they'd ambush us coming back, but the Cobras stayed right on top of us."

For a while they talked about Lieutenant Stafford. "How long will it be before he's back?" asked McCay.

"I don't know," Tilley said. "It'll be a while, and they may not even send him back."

The Marines were leaving. The list of those that had left was growing long. Seventh Motors, Force Logistics Support Group B, Ninth Marines, Third Marines, First Tank, Seventh and Ninth engineer battalions, Attack Squadron 223, Heavy Helicopter Squadron 361, All-Weather Attack Squadron 141, Fighter Attack Squadron 314. Could the Fifth Marines be far behind?

Men, at least these men, did not speak of these things. Just as they had not asked, why are we here? they did not ask, why were we here?

"I'm sending Lieutenant Hess to take over First Platoon," Captain Tilley said. "We're getting real short on officers and staff NCOs."

"Yeah, and we may lose our C.O.," said McCay. "How did the meeting go?"

Captain Tilley had been recommended for general's aide, and he had been called for an interview.

"OK, I guess," Tilley said. "What do I know about being a general's aide? I'm a line officer. This is all I know."

"Yeah, but it's a real opportunity," said McCay.

"It is if you don't foul up," Tilley said. "Knowing me, I'd foul up. What does a general's aide do? I had a buddy who was a general's aide once. He was an artillery officer and was acting as a forward observer for the Army. His radio operator kept yelling at him, but he was calling some grid coordinates and didn't pay attention, and a helicopter landed right on top of him. The rotor hit him on the head, knocked him unconscious, gave him a concussion, and when he came to he didn't know who he was for two weeks. If it hadn't been for his helmet, it would have killed him.

"That head injury really scared the Army, so they wrote up a medical profile that he was not fit to command troops, carry a weapon, or be assigned to a combat area, and they sent him back to the Marines. The Marines read his profile and nearly shit. What were they going to do with an officer who couldn't carry a weapon, command troops, or be assigned to a combat area? So they made him a general's aide.

"For two days he stood around not knowing what to do, so he asked somebody. They told him he was supposed to look after the general. How was he supposed to look after the general? Well, he looked around, and he discovered this little slit trench at the side of the general's hootch that was supposed to be the general's bomb shelter. It wasn't even deep enough to cover the general's ass, so he got a detail of men and had them dig it six feet deep. What he didn't know was that the general had hinges on the side of the hootch, and when there was a rocket attack, he just unhooked it and rolled out of bed, down the side of the hootch and into the trench.

"Sure enough, that night the siren went off, the general unhooked the sides of the hootch, rolled out of bed, and fell six feet into the bottom of the trench. He sprained his back and had to be taken to the hospital, and the next day my buddy was back commanding a line company. And he hasn't been promoted since."

We stood watching Tilley to see how genuine the story was, but Tilley was a poker player; his face told nothing. "Well, I'm going to get some Zs," he said. "I'm going to be up all night. Lieutenant Smith has his whole platoon out in the bush. They've been out all day, and they're going to stay out tonight. They'll draw some VC tonight and Blackhammer's coming back. You might see some fireworks," he said.

Captain Tilley went to get some rest, and I walked down to the helicopter pad, attracted by a strange sound at a combat base. It was the whine of a model airplane engine.

By the time I reached the pad, a small crowd of Marines had gathered to see a model biwing airplane fly. For a few minutes the owner entertained the crowd with loops and dives. "Crash it," some of the men called, and he dived the plane into the perforated steel plates of the pad. One wing sheared off, but it was not a wholly satisfactory crash. The builder picked it up and threw it on the pad. A wing broke but didn't come loose. He kicked it, and the other Marines ran out to stomp it to bits, pushing and shoving each other to be able to crush it beneath their own boots. When the airplane had been rendered unrecognizable, the builder said, "OK, let's get this mess cleaned up," and the wreckers policed up the scraps and carried them away.

"How long did it take you to build that?" I asked.

"About a month."

"Why did you tear it up?"

"I'm going home in a couple of weeks. I didn't bring anything here; I'm not taking anything home with me."

It was an attitude I had seen before. Vietnam was an aberration in their lives and they wanted no reminders. It was not an attitude I had seen in the CUPP Marines. In their minds were the villes and the faces of the peasants and PFs that they would carry with them always.

After a few hours of rest, Captain Tilley was back. "Let's go to the gunny's hootch," he said. "He has the best hootch here. He's the biggest scrounge in the Marine Corps."

A "gunny" is actually a "gunnery sergeant," one stripe below a master sergeant. Although officially the rank was changed to technical sergeant many years earlier, the tradition-loving Marines referred to such a man as "gunny." In the Marine Corps, the rank had a special reverence.

A Marine gunny was a singular breed of man. He was a "pro." He had been in the Corps a long time. He not only knew how to get things done by others, he knew how to do them himself. He not only knew how to do things by the book, he knew how to do things that were forbidden by the book. He not only knew how to put a second lieutenant in his place, he could represent the view of the private to the major. He knew there was a certain aura of respect for his rank, and he wore it with a kind of tolerant pride. He was expected to be a rugged individualist who could outshoot and outsmart anyone in the company, an eccentric who could chill a corporal or a second lieutenant with a glance, a raconteur who could entertain colonels or sergeants with sea stories and adroitly find moral lessons in the lies, a magician-technician who knew his way through the channels of red tape and around the desks of officious clerks, a father to the PFCs, and a buddy to the Old Man. He was supposed to be a character. Most of them were.

We sat in the gunny's comfortable hootch, which was equipped with two beds, chairs, a desk, bookshelves, an air-conditioner, and a refrigerator. None of this was standard issue. All of it had been scrounged by the gunny. The Marines regarded scrounging as an art form. Poorly equipped by Army standards, poorly fed by Navy or Air Force standards, any fat they had they scrounged.

There was another factor that made a scrounge desirable. It was an axiom of war that comfort remained in the rear. Officers' clubs and some NCO clubs used the freeze-dried shrimp out of Long Range Patrol rations as hors d'oeuvres. They were served without boiling or soaking and were eaten like popcorn. None of the grunts I talked to had even heard of them. In the bush, Long Rats meant chile con carne.

Another axiom of war was that the farther from the shooting, the bigger and more modern the weapons. The vaunted U.S. firepower was indeed overwhelming—in rear areas, where it was seldom manned. A hangover, no doubt, from Tet. It was not unusual for a line unit to be packing more mortars, machine guns, and recoilless rifles than they were authorized. The comfort and security of these weapons was provided by the company scrounge.

Captain Tilley and I sat in the gunny's comfortable hootch, awaiting the gunny's return. Tilley had sent him after thirty feet of communication wire. In ten minutes the gunny was back with a roll of wire.

"Jesus, I said thirty feet, and you've come back with a whole roll," Tilley said. "What did you do, steal it?"

The gunny was a large, hawk-faced man who limped with a steel brace on one knee. He looked at Captain Tilley with mock innocence. "I think I know where I can trade it for headlights for your jeep," he said. "You know someone stole your headlights."

"Who are you trading with, the VC?"

"The Koreans."

"Cut me off thirty feet of that wire, and get out of here before you get caught with it," Tilley said.

The gunny measured off a generous thirty feet of wire, cut it, and left with the rest of the roll. "I don't know what I'm going to do with that guy," Tilley said. "He's not even supposed to be driving a jeep with that knee. Hell, with that knee he's not supposed to be in the Marine Corps. They can't get rid of him, and we can't do without him.

"When the typhoon hit, it knocked out every generator at Baldy. The only power was the auxiliary generator at the Battalion Aid Station, and that guy was up in a tree in the damnedest rain and wind you ever saw, soaking wet, trying to tie into a twenty-thousand-volt generator. I said, 'Do you know anything about electricity?' And he said, 'I know everything about it.' We were the only people at Baldy, besides the hospital, that had lights."

For a while Tilley relaxed and talked of R and R in Hawaii with his wife. "It was really great," he said. "We got this helicopter to fly us to this little beach no one knew about. Helicopter was the only way you could get in. It cost me eighty bucks, but it was worth every cent of it. We took some food and poncho liners to sleep on, and for two days we didn't see anybody. We just lay in the sun or played in the water. For two days we didn't even put clothes on. God, it was great.

"What was really so wonderful was how slowly time passed. We didn't take a watch with us, and those two days seemed like a week. If we'd been in Honolulu the time would have just flown by. I would have been conscious of every minute. I couldn't have relaxed because time was going so fast. But on the beach we forgot all about time. I enjoyed every minute of it."

Captain Tilley sat quietly remembering and I didn't disturb him. Outside everything was quiet. Either I had got used to the 81mm mortars firing flares, or few were being called for. Neither of us spoke for a long time, and then we could hear the rhythmic beating that signaled the approach of the helicopters. "We'd better go," Tilley said.

Outside it was completely black. We felt our way to the jeep and drove to the Battalion Combat Operations Center. It was a large, windowless, sandbagged building, the nerve center of Combat Base Baldy. Besides the operations rooms, which took up one end of the building, there was a long corridor with offices and briefing rooms along each side. Leaving me in the operations room, Tilley disappeared down the hall.

The operations room contained banks of radios monitored by disinterested enlisted men and telephones manned by officers. In one corner of the room was a bank of radios and phones assigned to ROK Marines. Nothing much seemed to be going on. Above one of the desks was a sign: "The helicopter is the world's best substitute for proper planning."

In a few minutes Captain Tilley returned, and we went to a briefing room and sat down with the helicopter pilots. With the exception of a major who commanded Blackhammer, they were young men and looked like college students. Only a short time ago most of them had been college students. I was handed a card on which to write my name and medevac number and was introduced to the pilots.

"Is this guy going to stay for the whole ride?" one of the pilots asked Tilley. He turned to me. "We had a correspondent with us last week. We made a run and came back to get some more fuel and rockets, and the guy got out of the chopper. I thought he had gotten out to take a piss, but when we got ready we couldn't find him. We never did see him again. He just took off. He missed all the action too."

I made a vow to myself to stay to the end.

A ROK captain stopped in the doorway and looked in. He had the tough, solid look of most of the ROK Marines, and in his camouflage tiger suit he looked professional, military, and deadly. One of the U.S. officers spoke to him in a language I didn't understand. "I don't understand," the Korean said in crisp English. The officer spoke again. "That isn't Korean, that's Japanese," the Korean said, his tone indicating his attitude toward the Japanese. He turned and walked away. The Korean Marines practiced martial arts every day, and it was easy to imagine this one chopping down VC with his bare hands.

The briefing was brief indeed, conducted by a mustachioed captain. It was the kind of moustache a Marine captain ought to have—full and robust with just the hint of a jaunty curve at the end. He pointed out the areas the pilots would check and the positions of Lieutenant Smith's platoon and other friendly troops in the bush. There was a short discussion of the order in which the areas should be checked, and then the pilots looked at their watches.

"You've still got a lot of time. It's still early," the mustachioed captain said.

"Let's go get them," one pilot said, like a football player ready to get out of the dressing room and onto the field. The others agreed with an eagerness I had not been led to expect in Vietnam.

We went outside, got in three jeeps, and drove down to the pad. The helicopters were waiting. I was pointed to a chopper, the outline of which was barely discernible in the darkness, and was helped aboard. The helicopter was a Huey with an M-60 machine gun hanging in the open door on either side and rocket pods just behind the doors. An ammo can was placed for me to sit on. I was glad to have something to sit on, but a can full of tracers was not what I would have chosen.

I sat facing the two door gunners with my back to the armor plating of the pilots' seats, and tried not to think about a stray bullet hitting the ammo can. The floor in front of me was covered with ammo cases for the machine guns. One of the gunners, a slight, dark, handsome man I had mistaken for a pilot, handed me a sonic headset—two earpieces which cut out much of the noise of the whining engine but did not interfere with the normal range of the human voice.

The other gunner was larger and older. Fifteen years older. I was used to seeing middle-aged pilots, but a middle-aged gunner was a surprise. He pointed at the rocket pods just outside and behind the doors. "When they fire those things, they go right past the doors, and sparks and debris will fly in here, but don't worry about it, it's OK."

I made a mental note not to worry about sparks and debris flying about me while I was several hundred feet in the air, and got comfortable as possible on the thin, hard ammo can as the pilots started the whining rotors. The door gunners pushed forward an armored panel on each side of the helicopter. They were for the protection of the pilots and had been pulled back while the chopper was on the ground to permit the pilots to get in and out. After a few minutes of vibration we lifted off in a lazy spiral, circling over Baldy, so that I quickly lost all sense of direction. The night was totally dark, the sky as dark as the ground, so that the horizon was lost, and with it, reference to the ground. I knew the pilots must be flying on instruments. Below us I could see the red blink of Blackhammer's revolving anticollison light — the only light the helicopters were using. Flares hung in the air below us, but it was impossible to know which unit had fired them.

The middle-aged gunner tapped me on the knee. "Get ready," he shouted over the noise of the helicopter. "This is the first area. We're going to circle around and look." The helicopter seemed to turn in steeper banks now, so that the ammo box I was sitting on slid under my weight. I had been assured on earlier beltless, strapless flights that centrifugal force held me safely inside a helicopter. Did that hold true for ammo cans? I wondered if it was possible for me to slide right out the door on a steep bank, and, if so, whether I should grab for the machine gun, held in place with a pin, or for the gunner, who was wearing a safety belt. I decided to go for the gunner. His safety strap would hold both of us, and I didn't want to slide out into the night holding on to an M-60 machine gun.

"Stand by," the older gunner said. "They've picked up something." The searchlight popped on, and I followed its garish path along the ground, the trees looking flat and dead in the hot, white light. The light stopped on a hootch. It was amazing how clearly the hootch could be seen when separated from the blackness of the night. It was a masonry hootch with a red tile roof, and in the windows of the hootch were white flashes.

I thought at first of reflection of the searchlight off glass windows; then I remembered I had seen no glass windows in the bush. Muzzle flashes. At least three of them. Someone was shooting at us with automatic weapons. Before I reached my conclusion, the door gunner facing the hootch cut loose, and I could see not only his tracers but tracers from the other helicopters, which were in front and below us, converging on the target.

The tracers curved back in their downward path like water from a garden hose, and ricochets splashed crazily in all directions. I understood better the gunners' cliché of hosing down a target. It was hard to tell if they were on target, but it was difficult to believe all those bullets could miss.

The searchlight went off; the firing stopped. We continued to circle for a few seconds, and then the searchlight came on again, on target, but coming from a different position, and the machine guns opened up. Tracers came not only from our machine gun but from below and in front of us. I was certain we were going to collide with another helicopter or be shot down by their machine guns.

We went into a climb, banked sharply, and turned into a rocket run. It was more of a glide than a dive, and I turned on the ammo can so that I could look out the front of the helicopter between the two pilots. At times it seemed we were diving through the tracers of the other helicopters as they continued to circle and fire. I wondered if everyone knew what they were doing or if this was an inexperienced, cocky, and excited crew.

Using the crosshairs marked on the Plexiglas windscreen, the pilots lined up the helicopter on the hootch and opened fire. The rockets had a kind of roman-candle sound except that even through the headset they were a thousand times louder. Sparks, paper wrapping, and blasts of hot air blew through the back of the helicopter. I watched the rockets head for the ground trailing sparks and burst in a shower of stars. Then the noise of the rotors changed pitch, and the helicopter seemed to strain and shake as it pulled out of the glide and began to climb.

The older door gunner tapped me on the shoulder to gain my attention. "I wish we were using willie peter rockets," he said. "They are really pretty. They make a big splash of sparks." I didn't know whether he was worried about my entertainment or his own.

I had started the night with the suggestion of a headache way back behind my ears, somewhere at the back of my neck. I had thought it might pass; it had not. In the tension and noise of the takeoff, it had become full blown. The circling, noise and smell of the rockets, and changing gravitational forces of the glide and pullout had my head throbbing.

Blackhammer kept the hootch spotlighted, and whenever the gunners got a clear shot, they fired on it in seeming disregard of the helicopter making rocket runs. We turned in a tight bank and glided in again, seeming to fly right through tracer fire. But this time I knew what to expect.

After the pilots had expended their rockets, they made runs with the four machine guns under the belly of the Huey. For some reason, the sustained rattle of the machine guns was worse than the banging of the rockets. I thought my head would explode. The helicopter vibrated from the recoil of the machine guns, and I realized I was gritting my teeth from the pain in my head. I loved flying and had piloted private airplanes, but for the first time I thought I was going to be airsick.

I wondered if I should vomit in the camouflage bush hat I was wearing to avoid turning the floor of the chopper into a slippery mess, or whether I should try for the door with the chance that the slipstream might blow it back on the gunner. The helicopter pulled up with more straining and shaking and leveled off. The door gunners began straightening up the ammo boxes.

"We're going back for more rockets," the younger gunner yelled at me. Then he picked up a linkage from the belted ammo that had fallen in the ammo can. "That's what was jamming the guns," he said. Unknown to me, both guns had jammed during the attack. One of the falling links had struck me on the leg, but this time I had guessed what it was and hadn't thought I was wounded.

In a few minutes we were back on the pad. It was so dark that just getting out of the helicopter was a problem, as I couldn't tell how far it was to the ground. I half fell out of the chopper, sending a shock up my spine to explode in my head. I stood for a moment beside the helicopter, trying to swallow the contents of my stomach, thinking of disappearing into the darkness like the previous correspondent.

"How do you feel?" asked the pilot, a tall, blond, sleepy-looking man I had earlier mistaken for a gunner.

"I've got a headache," I said.

He climbed into the back of the helicopter, opened a first-aid kit, and gave me a pill and a canteen of water. The gunners were busy picking up rockets from a neat stack and placing them in the pods on the helicopter. I didn't expect much from the Darvon, but buoyed by hope, I gave the gunners a hand.

The long rockets, which the gunners called "nails," were not heavy, but I gingerly picked up one and carefully handed it to a gunner, who placed it in the pod. The safety pins were still in place, but I didn't want to drop one. The gunners were more at ease with them and handled them as though they were machine-gun barrels. Once the pods were filled we got back in the helicopter and lifted off.

"It isn't going to work," I told myself. "The pill isn't going to work." But already I could feel the tension in my neck and the back of my head beginning to loosen its grip. In a few minutes we were back at the hootch we had previously attacked. Blackhammer switched on its searchlight and bathed the hootch in light, but there was no answering gunfire this time. We circled around it again, the gunners at the ready, but nothing happened. "No bodies," the young gunner yelled at me. "Unless they're buried under the hootch." The hootch itself was a shambles. It was hard to believe the men firing from inside the hootch could have gotten away.

We left the hootch and flew to the next area and began to circle. The searchlight came on again, this time sweeping across a rice paddy. The gunners opened fire, following the light with their tracers. "Two people down there with packs and rifles," yelled the younger gunner, whose gun was on the outside, away from the action. "I don't think we got them." I never did see them, although Blackhammer flew over the area again trying to pick up either the bodies or the men. There was no return fire and no sightings.

We left the area and followed Blackhammer in its search for targets. Twice we went back to Baldy for fuel. My headache was gone and I felt fine. For a while I enjoyed the ride and then I got sleepy. We had already been flying several hours. I was also cold in the altitude and early-morning air, and I huddled on my ammo can, not really watching anymore, although the gunners remained alert.

I moved very little, husbanding all my warmth in one tight knot, and almost dozed off. Then I glanced out the door of the helicopter. What I saw was a black mass rising above us. We were in the mountains and we were below the peaks. I was instantly alert, wondering how well the pilots could see and how close we actually were to the cliffs that seemed within arm's reach. I turned to face out the front between the pilots' shoulders, and it seemed to me we were going to disappear into the mass of the mountain before the pilots turned away. Voluntarily my mind recalled stories of helicopters hitting mountains.

Seeing me move around, one of the gunners tapped me on the shoulder again. "There's a .51-caliber machine gun up here somewhere," he yelled. "We're looking for it."

The drowsiness left me completely. I had heard OV-10 pilots talking about encountering .51 machine guns. They marked them on the maps and left them for artillery or fast-moving jets to destroy. No Huey was a match for a .51 caliber, and for all I knew, we might be on top of it. We continued to circle, and each time it seemed we would fly into the mountain peaks before turning.

"That's it, we're going home," said the younger gunner in obvious disappointment. "Nothing happened tonight." The gunners cleared their guns, sat down, and lighted cigarettes, shielding them in cupped hands against the stream of wind through the chopper. I huddled on my ammo can shivering. No one had mentioned you could freeze to death in Vietnam.

Back on the pad, I shook hands and said good-bye to three of the helicopter crew. Each of them apologized for the lack of action. It was an attitude I had encountered before. They knew there wasn't much of a story without shooting and dying, and when it didn't happen they apologized for it, or they held out hope. "We'll get ambushed going back."

There was something poignant about battlefield good-byes. I had known those three men for ten hours. The copilot was always busy with checklists and radio communications and I never spoke to him. The other three I would not recognize if I saw them again, having seen them only in darkness. Most of the time conversation had been impossible. I knew nothing of them, nothing of their homes or lives.

But there was something personal and sincere in that good-bye. We had shared a moment together, a moment they would relive with minor variations on subsequent nights. But our good-bye had that special quality known to strangers who had shared a gear-up landing, had spent a night side by side fighting a raging fire, or had shared an automobile accident.

I would never see them again, never know which ones made it safely back to the world. Yet I would remember a middle-aged gunner who didn't want me to be startled by the blast and debris from the rockets and who was worried that I might not enjoy the show. And a young handsome gunner who cheerfully informed me that we were looking for an antiaircraft gun. And a sleepy-eyed pilot who asked how I felt, when he must have had other things on his mind.

Captain Tilley, the mustachioed captain, and I rode back to the Golf Company area. "How do you feel?" Tilley asked.

"I'm freezing to death," I said. "And I bet there isn't a heater in Vietnam."

"I've got a heater in my hootch," he said.

We adjourned to Tilley's bare-board hootch, where he produced a bottle of Jack Daniels which he poured generously into stained coffee cups. We sipped at the liquid, slowly getting warm.

"Did you see those guys shooting at us?" asked the mustachioed captain. He had ridden in one of the helicopters for fun.

"I didn't worry about those guys as much as I did our own gunners. I think one time the tracers were coming right through the door of the chopper," Tilley said.

"What really worried me was flying around in those mountains. Jesus, we were going right up the canyons. If the cliffs don't get you, the NVA will. They could have knocked us down with slingshots," said the mustachioed captain.

"Yeah, I think I recognized some of those places," said Tilley, who had fought in the mountains. "I think I saw the spot where we bivouacked one night. Right in the middle of a minefield. We had been humping all day, and when we stopped, everybody just fell where they were. It wasn't until a couple of hours later, when people began moving around and tripping them, that we knew it was a minefield. We just told everybody to stay where they were and not move until daylight, when we could see to get out of it. They started dropping mortars on us the next morning. That's when I got hit."

The two captains talked about the mountain fighting earlier

in the war when the NVA units were fresh and at full strength. "Those guys were good," Tilley admitted. "You met Sergeant Dignam. When he first came here he said he thought he had seen me before. He said, 'Were you in Operation Union? That's why I remember you. It was your company that came and got us.'

"His company had run into the God damnedest ambush you ever saw up in those mountains. They were surrounded and chopped to pieces. I heard the radioman die. I was talking to him and I heard him die.

"We were sent in to get them out. It was night, and we walked up the hill on a line, two men up and one back. We got our first kill with a bayonet. Charlie was facing up the hill, firing, and he didn't even hear us coming. When we broke through there were only nine men left fighting, and Dignam was the only one that wasn't wounded. He didn't even have a scratch.

"We dug in for the night, and the next morning a few people came straggling in. They had been overrun during the night and had hidden in the bush. One Marine came in just babbling. He was out of his head. His buddy had him by the collar and was leading him around. The gooks had chased them all night, but that guy stayed with his buddy and brought him in.

"They called themselves 'The Walking Dead of Delta.' 'Everybody in Delta is dead,' they said. 'We're dead too, but we're walking.' Dignam went through that without a scratch and got hit by a booby trap," Tilley said shaking his heaad. "He's going to be all right though. Just a broken ankle. He's a hell of a good man."

For a while no one said anything. I sat, letting the warm liquid course through my veins and chasing the chill from my bones. I could feel my muscles and nerves relaxing. The buzzing from the noise of the helicopters was beginning to leave my ears. Maybe the two captains were feeling the same thing I felt, wondering what it had been like with Delta in the mountains. Wondering what Dignam had learned about himself that night. Wondering how he felt when he saw rescue coming. Wondering what it was like to go back to Vietnam after that. Wondering what he and the other survivors of Delta had to say to each other.

"Name me a hero," Captain Tilley said, so suddenly I was startled. "There have been a lot of heroes in this war, but I bet you can't name one of them."

I couldn't. I couldn't imagine an act that would have made a man a hero to his countrymen. Killing any number of VC, as Sergeant Waitulavich had done, wouldn't do it. That kind of heroism belonged to an age when men went to the movies to hiss the enemy and applaud his death. Saving any number of friends or civilians wouldn't do it.

I had seen the driver of a Sea-Land van that had lost its brakes coming down from the Hai Van Pass drive his truck into a rice paddy to avoid hitting civilians in Lang Co. I had been to Camp Baxter, named after an Army truck driver. Baxter, wounded in an ambush, had driven his flaming five-thousand-gallon gasoline tanker off the road and over an embankment to his own death to avoid blocking the road to the convoy behind him. I couldn't imagine a greater act of heroism, but probably no civilian outside his family had ever heard of Baxter. Certainly those two life-saving acts were not celebrated by those who wore love beads and talked of peace.

"Name me a victory," Tilley challenged. "We haven't lost a battle in this war, and not one civilian can name a single victory."

I couldn't think of one.

"Khe Sahn," Tilley said. "That was the biggest victory we've had. And Tet of '68. But everybody back home thinks we got our ass kicked.

"We keep that road cleared for a year and nobody mentions it, but let one truck get blown up, and it's in all the papers that we failed. We keep those villes so quiet the villagers can sleep in their beds at night and no one reports it, but the VC massacres Thanh Binh, and it's a big victory for them. No one says they bombed civilians or burned their houses, but that's what they did. They killed a hundred women and children and it's a big victory. How many people protested that? How many pacifists called that a war crime?"

"Not a damn one," said the other captain. "There are two kinds of Vietnamese out here. The ones we kill are peace-loving farmers. It doesn't matter whether they are carrying rifles, grenades, mines, or what the hell, they are innocent civilians. But the Vietnamese the VC kill are corrupt officials or lackeys of the American military, it doesn't matter if the guy is carrying a rifle or a handful of buffalo shit."

The two captains leaned back in their chairs. It was late, and they were tired and a little worried about what I might write. After all, I could quote the mustachioed captain as saying, "The Vietnamese we kill are peace-loving farmers."

I tried to look friendly and understanding, but there wasn't a lot of trust between the military and the press. The military thought the press lied in order to report everything in the worst possible light and to accentuate mistakes and failures. The press thought the military lied in order to present everything in its best possible light and to cover up mistakes and failures.

The military believed that it had won victories—major victories such as Tet and Khe Sahn and Hue—that the enemy regarded as American victories, that the Vietnamese populace regarded as American victories, but that the media presented as defeats or, at best, Pyrrhic victories. The problem was that no one had ever come up with a good definition for "military victory." Certainly no one had defined what was a military victory in Vietnam. Back in the world newspapers were editorializing, "Say we won and come home."

Maybe Americans had seen too many wars that we "won" turn into peace that we "lost." Maybe *military victory* was an oxymoron, and all military actions were defeats no matter which side was declared victor.

"You guys are OK when you're not working," the other captain said. "It's that professional ego. You all think the war is run for your benefit."

I thought of the time the commandant of the Marine Corps had come to Da Nang. He was going into the bush to visit a line unit, and almost every reporter at the press center wanted to go along. The Marines arranged for the helicopters, but the morning of the visit, the unit in the field came under heavy attack. The commandant went, but the Marines canceled the helicopters that were to take the press.

The Marines said that the helicopters would be an attractive target for VC gunners, who would throw everything they had at them. Some of the reporters called MAC-V to complain, and some complained to their sponsoring organizations. Some tried to organize a boycott of the commandant's press conference when he returned from the field.

I didn't support the proposed boycott because I thought the Marines' explanation was a reasonable one. But the reporters' demand was not an unreasonable one. The commandant's presence in the field was news, and it was their job to cover it.

Captain Tilley tried to defuse the conversation by talking again of the private beach where he and his wife had spent R and R. "That's what you ought to do," he told the other captain. "Get your wife to meet you in Honolulu. I'll give you the name of the helicopter pilot. You just lie there in the sun. Don't take a watch. Just forget about time. If I'd had a watch I'd have gone out of my mind counting how much time I had left."

I wasn't really listening. I was wondering if I had gotten too close to these men, had become too involved in their routine to evaluate them by some objective standard. They were brave young men. And vain, as brave young men are. I was proud to have known them.

If I had been living with and writing about antiwar demonstrators, I no doubt would have liked and admired them just as much. And if I had been living with and writing about the Viet Cong, would I have admired them? Probably. It's easy to admire dedication. That's what makes single-mindedness so terrible, and why it strikes us with awe.

But these young men were not dedicated to war. They were dedicated to doing the job their country had given them. They were dedicated to serving a year and going home to the job and girl and classroom they had left. No doubt they would sometimes remember this year and the ville, the PFs, the Viet Cong, their buddies who died and were remembered and who lived and were forgotten. They would remember and wonder what it was all about and what it was to mean in their lives.

We sat, tired, sleepy, but still reluctant to give up the moment. "Well, what do you think of the program now?" Tilley asked.

I tried in the light of the Jack Daniels to add it up and put it all together. The children of Thanh Binh slept securely because the Americans were there, and the children of My Lai would never wake because the Americans had come. I thought of death by rules of engagement, conduct of fire, and friendly overlay. Death by booby traps planted by women and children and aimed at any living thing—pig, child, or Marine—that walked along a footpath. Death by electronic equipment in the sky that detected physical movement and animal warmth. Death by rockets aimed at population centers and bombs planted in market-places.

It wasn't a noble war. Noble wars existed in the minds of speechmakers and songwriters.

I thought of the stories I had heard back home before I came to Vietnam. Of the pacifist who hoped the war would go on forever in the same way because of the pleasure his moral righteousness gave him while costing him nothing. Of the preacher who gloried in the death of every Communist because the war was a crusade that should last until all evil had been napalmed.

There was some comfort and security in those absolute but simple views of the world. There was precious little in vaguely hoping for peace and freedom for the peasants in the villes. Captain Tilley's question remained. Was it a waste?

"I hear the Marines are pulling out," I said. The Vietnamization of the war was in the air. In Saigon and Da Nang everyone talked about the Americans' leaving. I had heard no one in the CUPP mention it, although it was clear that they were going. These men did not want to talk about it.

"We can't all go," the other captain said. "Somebody's got to stay behind and pick up the barbed wire."

What would happen to the PFs when the Marines were gone? Were they being weaned or abandoned?

"They'll fight," Tilley said. "They can keep the Viet Cong out of their villes. But they don't have any equipment. They don't have radios or artillery or even machine guns. They don't stand a chance against mainline NVA units."

Everyone knew NVA units were hiding in the mountains. Chased there by the Marines, they were waiting for a chance to come back.

What would happen to the villes? To the people who had invited the Marines into their homes, to their tables?

No one seemed to know. No one seemed to have thought about it. At least no one back in the world, in the streets, on the campuses, in the White House, or in the Congress seemed to have thought about it.

"I've got to be up in two hours," Tilley said, looking at his watch. For a moment he fingered the scar on his belly and stared into space. "A man has to be crazy to do this," he said.

Postscript

The war would continue for four more years. The killing would go on. But the protest was over. The cameras were going home. Tilley's question—Was it a Waste?—when asked, was on an inside page. And no one bothered to answer. Maybe only the peasants in the villes knew for sure.

Maybe Tilley, Waitulavich, Goyette, Roseberry, and the others weren't heroes. Maybe in our complex world there was no longer a place for heroes. Whatever they were, they weren't crazy. And we needed them.